PRAISE FOR
SWAGGER

"There's the 'fake it 'til you make it' crowd, and then there's the crowd with real and raw swagger. If you want to show up in the world in a powerful way, read this book."

TODD HERMAN, author of the *Wall Street Journal* **bestseller** *The Alter Ego Effect*

"Leslie Ehm's no-nonsense, tell-it-like-it-is approach shows you how to embrace your supposed imperfections as your greatest differentiator. Her book will help you get to the heart of your unique swagger, and prove that if you show up as exactly who you are, you will succeed."

ANDREA WANERSTRAND, PCC, global coaching programs leader, Microsoft

"Like a best friend, *Swagger* will help you step into your true potential and learn how to make the most of every single opportunity. Leslie Ehm shows you exactly how to lead yourself, tackle the chaos, and embrace the beauty of a life well lived."

PHIL M. JONES, bestselling author of *Exactly What to Say*

"Think swagger is about being brash? Think again. Leslie Ehm shows that true swagger unlocks generosity, confidence, focus, and impact ... and that's everything."

MICHAEL BUNGAY STANIER, author of the *Wall Street Journal* **bestseller** *The Coaching Habit*

"There is a badass inside you, just waiting to take over the world. All you need is a little swagger to release it. Buckle up and get ready for Leslie Ehm's no-holds-barred lessons to help you not just find your power but own it, too."

LAURA GASSNER OTTING, author of the *Washington Post* bestseller *Limitless*

"Tough mother love beautifully wrapped with moving examples, fantastic tips, brilliant storytelling, and wonderfully placed F-bombs. This book is the real deal in the art of being real. Leslie Ehm calls it *Swagger*. I call it brilliant."

RON TITE, author of *Think. Do. Say.*

"Some people believe you either have swagger or you don't. As a former rock star, that is *exactly* what I believed. After reading *Swagger*, I see that I was categorically wrong. This book will help you shake off what's blocking you, and reveal your one-of-a-kind awesomeness. Your inner rock star is waiting!"

BRANT MENSWAR, author of *Black Sheep*

"Warning! Reading *Swagger* may change the trajectory of your life. Leslie Ehm's book will open your heart and mind so you can open your own doors to success. If you're ready to reap the rewards of a more meaningful life, you need *Swagger*."

ERICA EHM, Canadian media icon and proud sister

"When we experience a genuine connection with a real human, we are captivated. When we learn to share it, we are freed. Leslie Ehm provides the key to unlock the cage containing our swagger. And that is f*cking awesome."

JAMES FELL, author of *The Holy Sh!t Moment*

SWAGGER

SWAGGER

UNLEASH EVERYTHING YOU ARE AND BECOME EVERYTHING YOU WANT

LESLIE EHM

PAGE TWO

Some names and identifying details have been changed to protect the privacy of individuals.

Cataloguing in publication information is available from Library and Archives Canada.
ISBN 978-1-77458-276-3 (paperback)
ISBN 978-1-77458-043-1 (ebook)

Page Two
pagetwo.com

Edited by Amanda Lewis
Copyedited by Steph VanderMeulen
Proofread by Alison Strobel
Cover design by Kelly Small and Page Two
Interior design and illustrations by Jennifer Lum

LeslieEhm.com
#SwaggerBook

For Russ, the finest human I know.
Thank you for always loving the real me.
My swagger is forever safe in your arms.

And for my mother, who never got to see this
but knew I had it in me long before I did.
Why not me, Mamacita?

> **❝**
> It takes courage to grow up and
> become who you really are.
>
> —E. E. CUMMINGS

> **❝**
> I had no idea that being your authentic self
> could make me as rich as I've become. If I had,
> I'd have done it a lot earlier.
>
> —OPRAH WINFREY

CONTENTS

PART ONE
WHY SWAGGER MATTERS

PART TWO
WHAT'S BLOCKING THE REAL YOU?

PART THREE
DRIVING THE REAL YOU INTO THE WORLD

PART FOUR
WALKING, TALKING, AND FEELING YOUR SWAGGER

PART FIVE
LIVING YOUR BEST SWAGGER LIFE

PART ONE

WHY SWAGGER MATTERS

1

WHAT IS SWAGGER?

IT'S NINE O'CLOCK on a Tuesday morning and I'm standing in a nondescript training room. A group of ten men mill around, darting slightly nervous looks at each other and smiling tentatively at me. A few wander over to introduce themselves, and it's firm handshakes all around.

We're about to start one of my presentation skills workshops. But these suited financial services execs have no idea that shit's about to get real up in here.

To kick things off, I list my credentials and experience. Former singer, TV host, advertising creative director, now entrepreneur, training professional, and coach. "I'm the Chief Fire Starter at Combustion," I explain. "It's my job to blow shit up." I tell them that this workshop is not just about becoming a better presenter; it's about learning to be comfortable with discomfort, finding their authentic voice, and keeping it real.

I ask, "Who wants to go first?" and imagine testicles shriveling. I smile warmly—the "mother" part of the "tough mother love" I'm known for. I wait. I've seen this scenario countless times: a group of senior executives taken out of their natural beige corporate habitat and thrust into the dreaded "skills building" scenario. By definition and design, this scenario is guaranteed to evoke a fair bit of insecurity. Add to that a small feisty woman who doesn't seem to fit the mold of trainer they're used to. Little do they know this will be unlike any training experience they've ever had.

I keep waiting.

Finally, one guy's hand goes up. Burly build, salt-and-pepper hair, open suit jacket. "I'll go," he offers. His smile does not disguise his reluctance. Straightening his jacket, he heads up front.

"Hi, I'm Tony."

"OK, Tony. Just pull a little paper strip from that cup and use what's on it to start telling us a story while I make some notes on how you're coming across," I instruct.

And he's off to the races.

I don't listen to a word. Instead, I focus on everything he's working incredibly hard not to show me. I watch how his energy and bluster amp up. He clenches his fists and juts one finger out on each hand, pistol style, as he jovially rapid-fires his way through his presentation. The fear around his eyes is in direct contradiction to his wide grin. He struts back and forth as he tells his story, a "good-time Charlie" all the way, voice booming, wearing his arrogance like a shield. And he doesn't fool me for a second.

Mid-sentence, I put my hand up to cut him off. He smiles expectantly.

"What the *hell* was that?" I say.

The smile falters a little.

"What was all of *this* bullshit?" I ask, mimicking the finger-pointy gun thing.

The smile droops. The room gets very, very quiet.

"Tony," I say, "despite you trying to distract from just about everything interesting and human about you, here's what I saw." His breathing hitches and becomes heavy. "You're the kind of guy who might have the cottage next to me up at the lake," I say. "One morning at five, I get up to go fishing, only my boat won't start. So, I go next door and wake you up. Are you pissed? Hell, no. You come out in your T-shirt and boxers and get my boat started. You might even come fishing. Am I right?"

Bewilderment overtakes Tony's reddening face. "How do you know that?" he asks. "Just from what I did?"

"Because I *see* you," I say. "Now cut the shit. I want you to talk about something you care about. Look me in the face and tell me the truth. Are you ready?" Tony nods. I count him down, 3...2...1. He opens his mouth like a fish a few times and inhales deeply. Finally, he starts talking, his eyes firmly on me.

"My mother... my mother..." he says. Then, the most guttural sob imaginable bursts out of him. He clamps his hand over his mouth, looking horrified.

"Keep going," I encourage.

"My mother was born in Italy and came here before she had me," he continues. His eyes start to fill with tears and, sobbing again, he turns his back.

"Tony... keep going," I say quietly.

He does. Tony tells us the story of his incredible mother, a tiny Italian immigrant who raised him with ferocity and love and was key in forming him as a man. As his story unfolds, tears stream down his face. One of the other guys gets up and hugs him mid-sentence. Tony goes on to reveal that his mother recently passed away, and now he feels a piece of himself is missing.

When he's done, the room of bankers gives him a standing ovation. Tony looks shocked. I go over and throw my arms around him. He hugs me back and whispers over and over, "I don't know what happened... I don't know what happened."

"I do," I say. "You just found your swagger."

Well, after that display, Tony was never again looked at the same by his colleagues. He was mocked, ignored, and undermined, and his leadership prospects went down the crapper, and—

Seriously? Did you really think that could happen just from being both brave and vulnerable at work?

I bet that while reading Tony's story, some of you were dying inside, thinking that if it had been you, you would never have shown your face at work again. But I also bet you were moved by his authenticity. Yes, Tony's work life changed that day, but not for the reasons you imagine. In one small but significant moment, Tony lost his fear and was able to be his real self. He was finally seen for the complete, complex, and messy human that he is—and *nothing bad happened.*

**Swagger is not about perfection.
It's about being a flawed badass.**

There it is. The fundamental dichotomy of the number we do on ourselves in the business world. We want to have what we think traditional swagger is—an air of powerful, cocksure confidence, no matter the situation. We want to be heard, respected, recognized, and rewarded for being our true selves at work, but we're too shit-scared of the possible repercussions. So, we squash our realness down, telling ourselves that we'll get what we want in the end if we're hardworking drones who don't stand out too much. After all, no one likes a "loudmouth," a "show-off," a "shit-disturber," an "upstart," or a "rule breaker."

Except that's bullshit. Because being real does not, by definition, make you an asshole. But it can make you a game changer.

I see this paradigm at play day after day in the "corporate jungle." And it doesn't matter how "cool" the company is. I've worked with them all: Google, TD Bank, IKEA, Uber, PepsiCo, Disney, Leo Burnett, and countless other corporate giants. They all have their culture of hierarchy, the rules of engagement, the game that must be played. There's always a uniform. It doesn't matter whether it's a business suit or jeans and a T-shirt: there's a way we're expected to show up, and we do. Why? Because we're afraid of what might happen if we don't.

And this doesn't change if you're an entrepreneur, part of a start-up, independent, or an aspiring *anything*. We *all* have an ideal stuck in our heads, and we spend our days thinking that we suck if we can't live up to it. "If only I could … then I would …"

SWAGGER REDEFINED

This is where I come in. I don't believe there's a prescribed way to behave at work if you want to succeed. Sure, there are social mores and HR-endorsed behaviors, but that's not what we're talking about here. I've spent the past decade getting paid to help people elevate their game, and there's one universal truth that surfaces time after time: the more you are able to be yourself in your work, the more successful you will be at work. That's what swagger really is. It's not about fronting or faking; it's the courage to do the complete opposite in the face of scrutiny or judgment.

Real swagger, new swagger, true swagger is *this*:

> *Swagger is the ability to manifest the real you and hold on to it in the face of all the psychological crap that's going to come for it—regardless of the situation or environment.*

Finding and liberating your swagger is a process that requires facing down demons, recording over old tapes, and challenging your own preconceptions of what you "should" or "shouldn't" do, say, and be. It's about taking new risks and seeing yourself differently, especially in a professional capacity. It's like living in an epic movie of your own making, with your own unique language, and never allowing other people to write crappy subtitles for you.

Swagger is not about perfection. It's about being a flawed badass. It's self-acceptance, not self-assuredness.

And once you find your swagger, you'll never, ever want to go back to who you were, because having swagger is the secret to that game-changing, next-level success.

In this book, I'm going to share stories of the countless people I've worked with and help you recognize the barriers to swagger.

Then I'm going to show you how to work through those barriers one by one. In my work, I've tried a million different approaches and techniques, had hundreds of one-on-one and group conversations, created exercises to produce kick-ass results, and kicked a lot of asses to get those results. I'm going to share my best approaches, techniques, and exercises with you so you can custom-kick your own backside and step into your swagger.

In lieu of you standing in front of me as we do this work, I have to imagine you are an amalgam of every gorgeously flawed, potential-filled, and powerful person I've ever encountered. Only you will know what resonates. But in the words of Oprah, *what I know for sure* is that something *will* resonate with you. Your job is to hear it and tell the truth to yourself. That's the first step in unleashing your swagger: no bullshit allowed.

Here's the thing: if you stop talking crap to yourself, you'll be less likely to talk it to anyone else. That includes negative or self-aggrandizing talk. You are not a loser; nor are you the king or queen of the freakin' universe. You are somewhere in between. And that's a beautiful and beautifully human thing. Depending on the day, you'll swing more to one end than the other and then back again. But what matters is your ability to accept where you feel you are, have a frank talk with yourself about why you're feeling what you're feeling, and then get your head right for the moment.

Getting to swagger isn't a switch you flip. It's a journey.

You've got this. And I've got you.

2

THE CASE FOR SWAGGER

WHEN I ASK people what they want to get out of training or coaching with me, it's usually that they want to "come across as more confident." It doesn't matter whether it's a leadership, creativity, or communication skills session—people just want to *look* like they know what they're talking about. It seems that we associate success with the illusion of having it all together.

Let's be real: we all marvel at those who can walk into a room and instantly command it. Their self-assuredness radiates off them in waves; they seem so effortlessly in command of themselves, and no one seems able to resist their peacock charisma.

If you google "How can I come across as more confident?" you'll find more than sixteen million results, including "7 Ways to Look Really Confident (Even When You're Not)," "7 Conversational Tricks to Appear More Confident," and "How to Fake Being More Confident When You're Just Not Feeling It." It seems we are so obsessed with looking badass that we're even prepared to lie about it!

There's a ton of research reinforcing the almighty power of a confident persona. Just one example: a University of Sussex study recently demonstrated that the "brain is wired to allow confident people to influence our beliefs.["1] Holy crap! Does that make the opposite true as well? No confidence = no credibility = no power of persuasion?

No wonder there's so much focus on developing a "swagger-y" front.

But what if you're going about this all wrong? What if the time you're spending to build the bullshit face of perfection you think the world wants and needs from you is actually getting in the way of achieving your real goal? And what if the outward appearance of swagger is just strut over substance, more "full of crap" than "full of confidence"? What if swagger is something altogether different than what we've been led to believe? It's time to shatter some of the myths that keep us from achieving true swagger.

THE CON OF CONFIDENCE

First, when it comes to having confidence, you either do or you don't. Despite what we've been led to believe, the "fake it 'til you make it" thing *does not work*. The worst fallout from faking it is that as soon as you go down that road, you have to keep going—no matter what. From the moment you pretend to know more than you do, you eradicate the opportunity to ask for help, and that will screw you every time. See, confidence doesn't breed competence; competence breeds confidence. How the hell are you going to get better and smarter if you don't ask and learn? There's brilliance in the heads of everyone around you just waiting to be tapped, and there you are, trapped in your "Nah, I'm all good" pretense. I've always put my money on telling others how much smarter they are than I am and then asking them to share their wisdom (ending the request with, "Oh, great one," usually seals the deal). Besides, don't we all secretly hate that smarmy jackass who claims to have all the answers? We know it can't possibly be true, yet we tell ourselves we need to be just like that to succeed. I call bullshit, and there's research to back me up.

According to Dr. Alex Lickerman, confidence is not about having all of the answers—it's about actually and honestly believing in yourself, which is very different from simply pretending to. In his book *The Undefeated Mind: On the Science of Constructing an Indestructible Self*, Lickerman explains there are three kinds of self-belief that ladder up to confidence: "belief in your competence, in your ability to learn and problem solve, and in your own intrinsic self-worth."[2] Did you notice that in Lickerman's view, confidence is totally based on self-perception? Even the formal definition of confidence found in the *Oxford English Dictionary* reinforces this emphasis on self-perception: "the state of feeling certain about the truth of something, or a feeling of self-assurance arising from one's appreciation of one's own abilities or qualities." Confidence is not a "thing" to get or achieve; it's a by-product of self-belief that stems from real competence. Fundamentally, if you believe that you are truly worthy of owning your awesomeness at the stage you're currently at, then you do. Nothing or no one can tell you differently. In that light, it makes sense to flip the adage from "fake it 'til you make it" to "feel it 'til you find it."

"Fake it 'til you make it" *does not work.*

There is a dangerous side effect of faking it, which a Cornell University research team called the Dunning-Kruger Effect.[3] If you start to believe your own hype without having the actual chops to back it up, you not only start making bad decisions, you also literally brainwash yourself into believing you're better than you are, which leads to less of a desire to improve. (We've all seen that happen in the world of politics, often with very dangerous results!) So while having some bravado might not sound like such a bad idea for your next team presentation, imagine the ultimate impact on your career. How long before you are labeled an arrogant or ignorant ass?

Even juicier still, a well-known study from the 1960s, which has since been replicated and proved, discovered that the way to make the best first impression and get people to like you is to screw up fast.[4] Yup, that's right. The phenomenon is called the "Pratfall

Effect." Spill coffee, make a bad joke, fumble, stumble, and recover—anything that makes you appear human and vulnerable will have a massive impact on how people are drawn to you. Our subconscious minds can't resist flaws in others because we all know how flawed we are. A senior advertising executive told me stories about how her team would purposely mess up their presentation when pitching a major piece of business to new clients. She discovered that the way the team handled and recovered from the mess was the key ingredient to being picked over slicker pitches. "They [the clients] would tell us they loved how relaxed and in tune we were with each other," she explained. "It made them want to be part of our family."

Humanity, vulnerability, and authenticity are the essence of swagger. Getting people to not just believe but accept and embrace this concept has been the biggest professional pain in my ass. I cannot tell you how many quality learning hours have been lost to chipping away at the "slick-o confidence" mythology. It blows my mind when people convince themselves that who they are couldn't possibly be good enough to impress. There's a term for that: "Imposter Syndrome." If you have ever stood in front of a room and believed that it was just a matter of time before someone cocked their head, squinted their eyes, stood, pointed, and yelled, "Wait a second. You don't know what the hell you're talking about . . . you're an *imposter*!" you now have a name for the terror. And the fear is real. No matter what level of expertise we actually have and how many times we've proved it, those of us who suffer from it will still quiver in our boots.

There's also a little biological issue at play. Our brains are designed to make us want to fit into our tribe.[5] Historically, if we were perceived as weaker than, different from, or a threat to tribal harmony in any way, the tribe's natural instinct was to oust us—or worse—lest we jeopardize the collective. While this instinct may have helped us survive back in the day, it's clearly no longer necessary in the same way. But the wiring is still in place, and if we don't challenge it, we succumb to the Star Trek "Borg," those cybernetic organisms linked in a hive mind, in lieu of our independence.

Most people are reassured by being able to identify with others. The fact that there's an "executive" in someone's title does not suddenly make their brain different from yours. In fact, once you get that senior title, you're even more desperate for the authentic human factor. Think about it. You have more people who rely on you and fewer with whom you can share your pain. There's more attention, focus, and pressure on you to bring out the excellence in the entire team. What's more likely to get you to your goal: bullshit to and from your people, or truth and realness from all of you?

Max, a Silicon Valley tech professional, describes swagger in a unique way. He says, "Two words come to mind when I dissect swagger into its constituent pieces—'hustle' and 'humility': the hustle to go after what you want and the humility to understand and appreciate that you aren't perfect, that you don't have the answers, and that you exist in so many ways of service to others. We don't often think about those two things in the same sentence, much less wrapped up in this word that gets so often associated with today's entrepreneur. Like, 'Wow, they've got *swagger*.' But that can translate into unchecked confidence. It's that bizarro version of swagger that is inauthentic, detached, and just sort of apathetic."

Amen to that!

REALNESS CREATES CONNECTION

Make no mistake. Reaching this point is not easy. For many, some kind of catalytic experience needs to occur before they'll actually buy into the swagger = authenticity paradigm. Often, these moments come accidentally.

One amazing woman I trained at a global bank told me about growing up as a child of Indian immigrant parents, and how she learned to fake who she was at a very early age as a survival mechanism. At home, Rohina was the good girl and cultural rule follower, but every day she'd throw off the conservative cloak, hitch up her skirt, smear on some lipstick and mascara, and play the role of bad girl that was expected of her in her urban high school. When she entered the male-dominated tech world, she felt the need to take on yet another persona: the tough woman who could bark with the big boy dogs. By her late thirties, she had little idea of who she actually was anymore. All she knew was that she didn't feel like herself, and she wasn't getting the recognition she felt she deserved.

When I first met Rohina in a leadership program, she was in a senior manager role and felt stuck—repeatedly, she was being passed over for promotions. She was frustrated as hell, and something had to give. I could smell her skepticism about my training program a mile off. Yet again, here was someone telling her to show up in a new and different way—only this time, she was being told to just be herself, which in her mind had never worked for her.

Her moment of truth came unexpectedly. Due to a scheduling challenge, she was thrust into the second part of the communication skills module—not with her peers but in a room filled with associate VPs, the very superiors who had been passing her over.

When I chatted with her later, she said, "I remember thinking, 'Oh, shit.' I knew this was going to be beyond scary for me."

Rohina was tasked with bringing something personal to a "corporate" story. She had a million options and about twelve back doors she could have exited through. Instead, she opted to open the door in front of her and walk through. She told us about being a "fat kid" and how the obesity had been her protective armor after her parents' painful divorce. She spoke from the heart, revealing fears and moments of sadness. For her, opening up in this way was a risk of epic proportions. She had never talked about this with *anyone*, let alone a room filled with people who held her future in their hands.

The impact was immediate.

"I felt the air in the room change," she said. "I realized that suddenly these folks had a very different perception of me. Because of the 'tough guy' suit I'd put on for work every day, I had created the illusion of never having gone through crap like this. After that, it was different. They were real with me, warmer, and they shared things about their own lives. It was just easier."

From that moment, Rohina found herself more connected. Hallway chats were more relaxed, and approaching leaders for face time became easier. As a result, her name started coming up more in talent conversations. "I went from being another keener to a player that day. I felt my own power—that I could be me and they'd like me.

"You know when you're a sellout, when you're faking it to make it," she confessed. "That's an intention, a decision, and it's fucking exhausting. But then I realized that if you drop it, they drop it, and the conversation totally changes."

> 66
>
> **When you step into your authenticity,**
> **the sky's the limit—it's boundless. Once you find**
> **your swagger, you will never, ever go back.**
> —ROHINA

Rohina was chosen to speak at the kickoff for a subsequent leadership program and held up as one of the super-successful candidates from the previous cohort. "They could all see me then," she said, "really see *me*, in my skin and with my own words." After that, she was able to sit down and have very different conversations about her career trajectory. The next time her name was raised, the question wasn't "why her?" it was "why *not* her?"

Soon after, Rohina was offered a new role as associate VP reporting directly to the chief technology officer. One perfunctory interview. No more being sidelined. It was hers for the taking.

"Because I knew that they had chosen the real me, I was able to stop replaying every conversation in my head after they happened and just use my energy to do great work. Now I'm in a space where I can just be myself every day. When you step into your authenticity, the sky's the limit—it's boundless. Once you find your swagger, you will never, ever go back."

I would never tell you that you'd be more successful by being your true self if I didn't absolutely believe it and hadn't seen it proved over and over again. That would constitute some kind of malpractice. And we can't take the next step together unless you believe it, too. I'm not saying you need to know how to do it (that's where I come in), but you need to want to, and you need to believe in the benefits. So take a second and answer the following questions with either an "agree" or "disagree"—it's like a BuzzFeed quiz for the Swagger Psyche.

Answer from a place of "anything is possible in a perfect world," as opposed to what your current reality might be. If you can dream your swagger, you can attain it.

1 If people really saw me for who and what I am, I think I'd be further along in my career.

2 I believe that most people are hoping for me to succeed rather than waiting for me to fail.

3 I could be far more focused and confident at work if I didn't feel the need to fake it.

4 My real-life personality is more interesting than my corporate front.

5 If I were more myself at work, I could be much more persuasive.

6 I'm a juicy human being with good intentions who deserves all good things.

7 I'm exhausted by the energy required to try to be someone or something that I'm not.

8 The people I respect most at work are the ones who seem the most honest, human, and accessible.

9 I'd rather be recognized and promoted in appreciation of who I really am than succeed because I was good at putting on a false front.

10 I don't need more of these obvious questions to prove that being anything less than myself at work is a really bad idea.

If you answered "agree" to any of these, you're a prime candidate for upping your swagger game. And the first step in getting there is believing that the journey will be worth it. So, congrats!

Let me recap the case for swagger.

- The confidence we so desire cannot come from faking it. Only competence can breed confidence. To have it, your shit has to be real or you will always suffer from self-doubt.

- As humans, we are drawn to authenticity. By definition, this is messy. The shinier we are, the less we evoke trust and connection.

- Accepting that we are works in progress gives us permission to ask for help to grow. Pretending we're all that and a bag of chips stunts our potential.

- Believing you're too much of a badass—that you're beyond reproach, super-cool, and more adept than you actually are—can lead you to make bad decisions and not even realize it.

- If you embrace swagger, show up as exactly who you are, and are still able to progress in your career, you will never have to pretend again.

Onward and upward, people. Let's get swaggering.

3

———

SWAGGER AND
THE REAL YOU

SO MUCH OF getting a handle on your swagger depends on figuring out who that truly authentic being is that's been trapped inside you for so long. Because if you can't see it clearly, then what the hell is it that you're supposed to be manifesting?

Not an easy question to answer. But it's always good to start with what I know for sure about all of you.

You are 100% unique. Comparing yourself to others is a waste of time. While this can feel like it's harder to pin down because there are no established rules and there is no perfect personification of what your true self might be or "should" look like, it's also pretty damn liberating to stop comparing. No one's true self is better than anyone else's. Being "your best self" is completely subjective. As humans, we are naturally messy, flawed, inconsistent, and reactive. So gazing adoringly at another human and envying their seeming charisma or personality can't be a measurement tool. Your version may manifest in very different ways. That's totally cool.

Authenticity begins with the alignment of how you think and feel with what you say and do. Truth time, reader. We all know when we're being full of shit, regardless of our reasons. We may not like it about ourselves, but we shouldn't hide from it. In fact, the opposite is true. Watching and listening carefully to our actions or what comes out of our mouths and comparing that directly with what we think or feel is a great way to determine how real we're being. Don't bother with the "why" at first. That will come later. But a fantastic first step is learning how much of a disconnect there is. You can't solve a problem until you know what it is!

Here's a little exercise to help with that.

---

1 Pick a scenario that you know triggers your bullshit. It could be from any aspect of life—work, relationships, day-to-day interactions with the world. Jot it down.

2 Write down what you would typically say or do in that situation. What would naturally and reflexively spring from your mouth or cause your behavior to change?

3 Write down what you would be thinking in those moments—those secret, private truths that scream on the inside.

4 Fill in what you would be feeling at that moment. What emotions would be bubbling up?

Try this for a few different scenarios.

Take a step back. Look at whether all of these elements are in sync—meaning, whether or not what you'd be feeling and thinking are completely aligned with what you'd be saying and doing. I'd lay dollars to doughnuts that the "say" and "do" answers are more representative of the false front you may be putting on, and that the real you, who remains stifled and silent, lies more in the "think" and "feel" answers. If so, you know you've got some realigning to do.

You don't always have to love the real you (nor does anyone else). See above. So-called imperfection is what often brings the flavor to the recipe of our uniqueness. The secret is accepting and even embracing it. Otherwise, we're trying to make ourselves vanilla. And I, for one, am not a major fan of vanilla. Give me spicy mocha choca double twist flava any day—even if it gives me mild heartburn on occasion. Besides, one person's pain in the ass may be another's role model.

There are no different versions of the real you. What you manifest should not be determined by where you manifest it. That's a key component of swagger. So if you're night and day at work versus play, then you know something's up. I'd also lay bets on the "play" version being closer to your true self. Sure, there may be nuances, but the fundamentals should remain the same. Don't let the world define who you are; instead, define yourself in relation to the world.

The real you is constantly evolving. You may feel that you are very different from, say, who you were five or ten years ago. Or you may see that you're just a slightly evolved version. Either way, knowing those differences and being able to track from then to now is a good way to understand who you actually are. We tend to let go of baggage over time so that the real us can be freer to move around. But we can also change to overcompensate for what we feel are flaws or failings. That's worth holding up to the light as well because it can reveal aspects of ourselves that we're unable to accept. There's a reason people in their later years are seen as more unfiltered and less concerned about what others think, and have a lower tolerance for others' bullshit. Growth is awesome, evolution is even better—but it should be with a view to best excavating who you are, not changing to please others.

From our words to our feelings, our self-image to our worldview, nailing down who we honestly are can be our life's work. But that doesn't mean we can't develop swagger around what we do know to be true to date.

WHAT DEFINES WHO YOU ARE?

Every single one of us comes into this world a swagger-filled badass. We're born fearless and curious, authentic and honest. And then life takes over and begins the slow, inexorable process of kicking the shit out of our confidence. It can happen in tiny degrees or all at once as a result of trauma, loss, or abuse (and sometimes we don't even notice *that* happening). Most of us can't pin the moment to an event or experience. We just realize that somewhere along the way, the world became a scary or inhospitable place and now we're struggling to swagger in it. So we become our history, a sum of damaged little parts that eat away at what used to be our "whole." We become the proverbial frogs that get boiled into submission, fear, self-doubt, or self-loathing. Who hasn't asked the question, "When did this happen to me? How did *I* get like *this*?"

I've found that trying to unravel this particular mystery is incredibly helpful in regaining swagger. It involves investigating what our environment told us, what the people closest to us said—intentionally or not. These messages become the tapes we play over and over and fucking *over* for years to come. Even those of us who know we were loved, who managed to escape trauma or abuse, can usually track back to the source of our issues, given some thought (and time, and counseling).

Complete this sentence:

In the past, I was always told that I was _____.

What was the overriding message you heard repeatedly that became the world's reflection of you—and that you ended up believing?

Here's my story.

I was raised by an awesome, epic mother. She loved me fiercely and seemingly unconditionally and told me I could do or be anything I wanted. But there was a catch. The way she said it (or the way I heard it, which is equally valid) went like this:

> *"Leslie, you're so smart. If only you could pay attention more."*

> *"Leslie, you're so funny and creative. If only you could control your emotions."*

> *"Leslie, you're so strong and fearless. If only you could dial it down sometimes."*

Over time, I stopped hearing the first part of the sentences. I became "if only"—a caveat. She was only trying to help me, give advice, and, yes, sometimes reflect what the world may have been saying about me, for what she believed was my own good. But here's what my sentence became: *"In the past, I was always told that I was too much and not enough."*

That's the tape that played throughout my entire life. I believed that no matter what I did, felt, or achieved, there was always that caveat, that "if only." So I never felt good enough. No matter what the facts were to the contrary, I believed that if only I were somehow different, I could achieve more or better. Worse, I believed that my accomplishments were despite my swagger, not because of it.

Have I mentioned how much my mother loved me? Making me feel "less than" was the direct opposite of what she wanted for me. But she was the loudest voice in my life, and I took my cues from her. If *she* thought this, imagine how the rest of the world perceived me? It didn't matter that she didn't mean it, or maybe she didn't even say it as often as I heard it. My developing psyche latched onto it as truth, and it became the story I told myself. The result was my believing that my truth and intention were somehow flawed, incomplete, or invalid. Being just me wasn't good enough; if only I could be something else. So much for self-belief.

With no direction or prelude, I get my workshop participants to complete the sentence I asked you to answer earlier. I never lead them toward the positive or negative. It's their choice. About 95% of the time, the statements are negative. And more often than not, it was their family who cemented their belief. For the record, almost all of them believe they were well loved by their families. They even defend them, citing culture as the influencer, or best intentions, or the voices of their own parents' families being repeated.

Growing up in India, Amaira was always told that she was "not good enough." In a family of four girls, she was the only one who had inherited the dark complexion of her father. As a result, her marriage prospects were going to be sketchy, at best. For her entire life, Amaira has believed that she is "less than" due to her skin color and that she will never be good enough simply because she isn't fair-skinned. To this day, she says she can't look at herself in the mirror for long, and she's become obsessed with trying to look perfect. For the record, not that it even matters, Amaira is a stone-cold hottie. Now, living in North America where the societal standards of beauty reinforce that, she still can't feel it.

Or there's Nazanin, who grew up in Iran. Her parents always told her that she was "too stressed and anxious." On the surface, that might sound like she was being told that she was putting too much pressure on herself. But we scratched the surface a little and realized that she was simply trying very hard to model the values and message she'd heard over and over again in her home: "Be great; accomplish things; prove your worth; you need to be better than everyone else in order to succeed..." The result? She was tied up in knots trying to be perfect in order to please everyone. And what did she hear? Criticism. "Nazanin, you're *too*..." How terribly sad is that? The same stress and anxiety are still alive and well today, but she's realized that she's been inadvertently sending the exact same message to her daughter—that perfection is somehow not just good, but necessary. So history repeats itself.

I have hundreds of stories just like these. They all represent the root cause of so much of our swagger-suck. I mean, if the people we trust the most tell us we're somehow not worthy, who are we to doubt it? Even the positive answers come with baggage.

Ellen's sentence read, "I was always told that I was loved." She was an adopted child in a family of four biological kids, so that message was critical to her sense of acceptance. As a result, she says she developed a great sense of confidence. But here's the rub. Turns out she was also living in a home where she was conditioned to never speak her truth in case it "made someone else feel bad." Ellen realized that this caused her to unconsciously believe that her thoughts and feelings weren't legit. She says it wasn't until she was in her twenties that she clued into the fact that her feelings were as important as anyone else's, and speaking her truth was actually allowed. So while she was constantly being told she was loved, she wasn't getting the message that she was free to express herself authentically. But c'mon—I mean, you're *loved*, so what's the big deal, right?

The point is, we're all affected by our past and what we believe to be the truth of what we were told—for good and bad. But it doesn't have to end there.

Read this next bit carefully. It's a mindblower.

You are not your history. You are the stories you tell yourself.

I believed that I was the walking manifestation of unrealized potential. Great, but still not good enough. But the second I decided to stop telling myself that old story, it ceased to be true. I could then start telling myself the story that *is* true for me now—today.

So comes the second part of the exercise.

Fill in this sentence:

Today, I'm always told that I am _____.

This sentence will be evidence of who *you* are now, today—who you've become and how you've used the past to your benefit. How what may have felt like criticism has turned into your strength, your purpose, your beauty, and, yup, even the source of your swagger.

Mine goes like this: *"Today, I'm always told that I'm incredibly passionate."*

The part of my history sentence that was actually true was that I was a lot of human. Big personality, big heart, big brain. Today, the world recognizes that part of me as being a gift, and no one ever tells me I'm not enough or I'm too much. Nor would I allow them to. Because I'm not my history. I am much, much bigger than that. And so are you.

**To accept where we've been
gives us the power to own where we are.**

When I get people to create their "today" sentences, they're amazed by how positive they've become. This is because, for the most part, as adults we remember the positive comments. We're trying to fix our damage and plug our holes. The positive goes in a little easier. The trick is to know how to hold on to it and let it inform and unleash our swagger. Our "today" sentence is the big *fuck you* to the negative voices in our heads. It describes the person we are learning to believe we've always been—the badass we didn't know we already were. And it's so much closer to the truth than our history is.

In her Netflix special *Nanette* (dir. Madeleine Parry), brilliant comedian Hannah Gadsby challenges a common comedy concept— that self-deprecation is funny and helpful—by suggesting that the negative words we say to and about ourselves can be a form of self-abuse. Comedians are known for this—using their stories as fodder for laughs no matter how painful the reality may have been. On the surface, it makes sense—to make light of our painful paths in the hope that it will take the sting out of them. But it doesn't work. Instead, what happens is that we end up disrespecting ourselves when we minimize what we've been through, how we transcended or used our past to make our present more meaningful. Gadsby sums this up so eloquently: "You learn from the part of the story you focus on," she says. "I need to tell my story properly."

If we want to live in a place of swagger and face down the barriers of pain, fear, insecurity, and more, we need to start by understanding where those barriers took root and how they grew. To accept where we've been gives us the power to own where we are. Best of all, doing this sets us up for a future that we can control. Once we do, then we have no need for a bullshit persona—we've stopped compensating (or *over*compensating) for what the voices in our heads keep chanting at us.

Fill in this sentence:

In the future, I want to be remembered for _____.

This is about looking at where you've been, seeing how you've evolved into who you are today, and then examining how you're going to use that truth as a superpower, both in and for the future. Think of it as the legacy you want to leave.

For me it is: *"In the future, I want to be remembered for how I was able to unleash human potential."*

When I look at my past perception of being "too much" and bring it into the present as "passionate," then it only follows that I can use that passion to do amazing things. I want to and can use the reality of my "hugeness" to do good in the world. But if I'd stayed stuck in believing I was my history, my ass would be dragging on the ground, mired in self-doubt and insecurity. To hell with that. I am not my history, and neither are you yours! Telling your story properly is a critical step in knowing and accepting who you are—and learning to be in your place of swagger.

Amaira figured this out. Her final sentence read, "In the future, I want to be remembered for having been more than just good enough."

She knows she's a work in progress, as are we all. But she's moving through her history to get to a future of being full and fully realized.

Don't we all deserve that?

FEELING LIKE A FAKE VERSUS BEING ONE

When going through the somewhat existential process of figuring out who we actually are, we will likely have questions about what is fact and what is fiction (of our own making). How does one distinguish the line between "being real" and "acting real"? What the hell *is* authenticity, anyway?

Feeling like a fake and being fake are two very different things. As we take on new roles or build our businesses, there will always be stages, interactions, and responsibilities that are totally foreign to us. If now you're a manager and you suddenly find you need to have a tough conversation with someone you used to vent with over drinks, it can seem totally, cringeworthily inauthentic, not to mention a little bizarre. In your mind, and based on prior experience, sharing a beer, hugging it out, or telling them to just "blow it off" might have been the best course of action. Now, you have to worry about how engaged they are, whether they'll be toxic to the rest of the team, or how to make sure they just get shit done. So instead of saying what you really *want* to say, like, "C'mon, dude, suck it up and pull your head outta your ass," you now feel like some weird HR-inspired zombie who has to gently probe for the root cause, provide context, be firm yet compassionate, and walk the legal line— while inside, your eyes may be rolling back in your head.

Let's say you're an entrepreneur who's never had to face down a supplier and challenge them on price or delivery time, and who has always felt that friendships are the best way to cement business relationships. The day you have to get heavy and call them out may make you feel like you're a different person completely. Let's not even get into selling—most people feel like they need to take a bath after a sales pitch. There are few things that feel less real than a spiel.

So, what's authentic? Giving that team member the one-two punch you think they deserve, which would have been your two-beer advice under the old auspice? Nope. Not in this situation. Or should you suddenly become some demanding diva and get all uppity with your supplier or vendor? Double nope.

The trick is figuring out what *your* version of these roles looks, feels, and sounds like. You have to put on different hats and then learn how to make each one feel authentically comfortable. And you will not get it right the first, second, or third time.

If our work environment has us running in circles of self-doubt, we can get pretty lost. On the one hand, we're encouraged to be ourselves, but on the other, we get smacked down if we're "too real." Authenticity is now considered a key leadership quality, but there's no handbook telling us what the hell that even means. If you're having a rough day and feel the need to run screaming through the halls in your underwear, railing at the world, could you simply chalk it up to having an "authentic moment"? Not bloody likely. There seems to be a very precarious balance between being honest and genuine and being an unfiltered shit show. You'd think the lines would be clearer. But every person, and every organization, has their own cultural tolerance for realness.

Nothing in the world feels better than keeping it real!

My brilliant, always quotable friend Ron Tite, CEO, speaker, and bestselling author of *Think. Do. Say.,* said this about authenticity: "We all have a range of clothes in our wardrobe. We have a certain suit for some occasions and a different set for the cottage. But they're ours. If we go out and *buy* a new outfit to impress someone, then we've lost our authenticity."

So, authenticity is more "how do I adjust my hat?" than going out to shop for a brand-new one. And you'll know if you've gotten the tilt just right not if it looks good, but if it *feels* good.

Because nothing in the world feels better than keeping it real!

PART TWO

WHAT'S BLOCKING THE REAL YOU?

4

SWAGGER BLOCKERS

EVERYONE IS CAPABLE of swagger. Being an introvert or inexperienced is no excuse. Conversely, just because you're a crowd-pleaser, show-off, or master of the "fake it 'til you make it" mentality doesn't mean you already have it. Tapping into and releasing true swagger has to be a conscious act. You won't always notice when, where, why, or how it's getting stuck unless you understand the psychological blockers holding it back. Imagine that the real, authentic you—the one seen every day by those who already love and accept you—sits at your very core. This is the you who feels free to speak and act without self-consciousness, fear of judgment, and constant nagging self-doubt.

It's the you that the world deserves to see because it's goddamn gorgeous and perfect in all of its messy, human imperfection. When the world accepts and celebrates the real you, your mind, body, and spirit can really feel it.

But it's also the most vulnerable you. If you show this real you to the world and are met with criticism or rejection, it hurts like a bitch. That's why most of us keep our true selves tucked away. So when the world slings arrows at us, we can argue that they're not really getting to our hearts. The problem is, if nothing gets in, then nothing can get out. We surround ourselves with layers of our own making both to defend against threats and in response to what we think the world expects from us. Together, they combine to make an *American Ninja Warrior*–style gauntlet that has to be navigated if we're ever going to achieve true swagger and manifest our badassness for all the world to see.

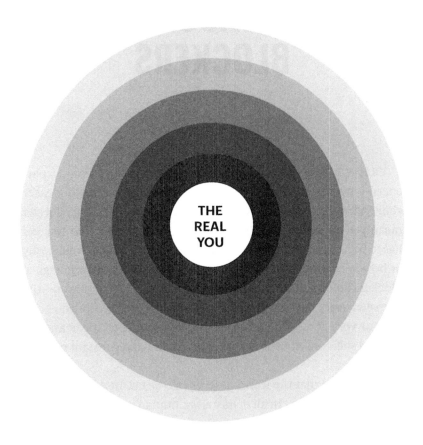

These layers are your swagger blockers, each one having a nasty way of reinforcing and validating the next. Only by identifying and understanding what they are, why they exist, and, most importantly, how the hell to get through them will you be able to drive your swagger through to release your one-of-a-kind awesomeness into the waiting world. And as you learn how to navigate these blockers, the real you will grow, gain momentum, and become powerful enough to face the world in all of its glory. In time, the blockers will lose their power and fortitude, and the real you will be able to flow in and out like a hot knife through butter. And that, my friends, is the swagger recipe for so much happiness, confidence, and, yes, even success.

So, let's face down these layers one by one and get on with the challenging but oh-so-rewarding process of getting your swagger on!

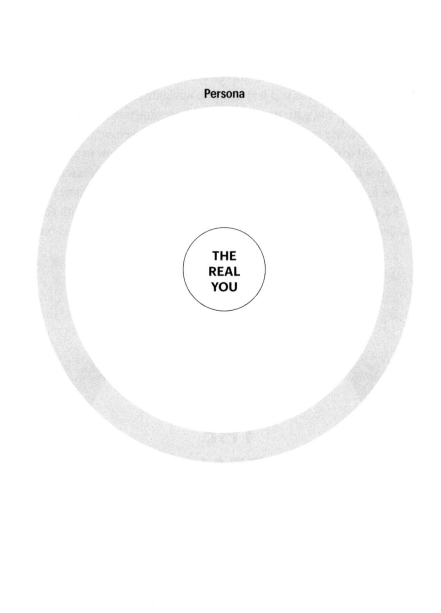

5

PERSONA

THE FIRST SWAGGER blocker separating the *real* you from the world is *Persona*.

So many of us develop a conscious demarcation between who we really are and what we reveal to the world, particularly in the context of our professional lives. We do this because we've been conditioned to believe that there's a way we're supposed to show up if we want to succeed. But the truth is, having a work persona does not help. It just hides our uniqueness and shrouds our value.

We tend to think we're the only ones putting on a front—and we're just doing it to create the illusion of being equal to others. Well, it's time to out the truth: almost everyone is fronting, just like you. It's a rare individual who feels comfortable enough in their skin to say, "Screw it. Here I am in my flawed glory for all the world to see." But those are the people we usually trust and respect the most. When we align our persona as closely as possible with our true self, we can step into our power big-time. And I mean *big*-time! Only when we officially stop pretending that we're perfect can we start a meaningful evolution to become better humans and ask for help along the way. By exposing persona for the illusion it is, we can begin to fly our beautiful freak flags high and show the world who we *really* are. Ain't *that* a relief?

SEPARATING THE PERSON FROM THE PERSONA

Imagine that your best friend from tenth grade could watch you give a high-stakes presentation in front of a group. What do you think they'd say afterward? Would they recognize you as "you," or would they wonder what kind of corporate droid you've become, all dressed up, spewing acronyms and business buzzwords, and nervously scanning the room for approval? Honestly, they'd likely laugh and ask, "Dude, WTF?"

Good question. WTF? Why is it that we can't just be the same person at the office as we are at a bar with our buddies? What's the purpose of this coat of persona we put on every morning? We tell ourselves that it's contributing to our swagger by smoothing out all the rough edges, but that's just not true.

**When we align our persona
as closely as possible with our true self,
we can step into our power big-time.**

Persona is a kind of force field designed to project an illusion of being someone or something you're not. It's like having a perfect and impervious avatar who can go out into the world and protect you from the dangers of interaction. The word "persona" originated in the term for an "actor's mask," and that mask is hiding all of the messy stuff we really need to accept in order to release our swagger. Talk about a catch-22. If I can't reveal who I really am, I can't have the real me accepted. And if I'm afraid the real me won't be accepted, I create a persona as a stand-in.

I vividly remember when I was fifteen years old, crying to my mother about how the boys just didn't "get" me. I was venturing into my "alternative" years—slightly punky, not terribly girly, and as in-your-face as I am today. I told her I was thinking of changing it up so that guys might find me more attractive and acceptable. Her advice was brilliant and applies to every aspect of life—even today. She said, "If you pretend to be someone you're not in order to get someone to like you, it'll be only a matter of time before the real you is revealed. If you get rejected *then*, you'll be devastated because you'll have invested so much in the person. But if they don't like you from the get-go, it's not that big a deal. Besides," she added, "if a guy is too stupid to recognize what an amazing girl you are, why would you want to go out with him, anyway?"

Brilliant, right? You can swap "guy" for "job," "company," "client," and so on. Relying on something that isn't real in order to gain acceptance is a house of cards waiting to fall.

PERSONA NON-GRATIFYING

Let's stop the madness by digging into the concepts of "work you" and "personal you." I hear this argument for two selves a lot, which is grounded in a belief about what professionalism is and what it isn't. Professionalism is following the basic rules of your work environment: doing your work well; showing up on time; being discreet; never leaving colleagues hanging; being respectful of ethnicity, gender, sexuality—all of that important stuff. But there's *nothing* in that definition that requires you to wear a (metaphorical) mask. Unless you're a closet asshole who doesn't care a lick about playing nicely with others, you're pretty much good to go.

I've never seen a company handbook that started with, "In order to be happy and successful here, first you must assimilate into the Borg. Please walk, talk, dress, and interact as much like your colleagues as possible. Only then can you ascend to greatness." And if the handbook did say that, would you want to work there? Nope. But then you willingly make those exact choices yourself.

Think about all of the energy you channel into keeping your persona intact for eight hours a day. It requires you to make constant micro-decisions about how to show up—your language, work politics, and interactions. When to speak up and out, and when not to; how to dress and carry yourself; and how to find your social positioning. It's exhausting. It also requires a continual process of self-judgment. Ironically, we judge ourselves far more harshly than the world ever could.

There's another perceived layer of challenge around persona for women as opposed to men. I've encountered countless amazing, powerful women who believe they need to show up "like a guy" in order to be taken seriously. This is what Rohina did when she entered the corporate world, and we know how well that initially worked out for her. On the flip side, men worry that they can't ever show vulnerability if they're to be respected. Two sides of the same coin. It would be so much easier if we could all accept being authentic, complex human beings. Sometimes we're hard-asses, sometimes we're marshmallows. That's our truth. Knowing we're all stuck in the same conundrum, why not use the dichotomy as a way to insightfully empathize and connect with others? Embracing that is so central to what swagger is!

I'm all for having social savvy—meaning, fundamentally knowing what's appropriate behavior in different situations. (No, do not throw down that breakdance challenge to the boss's wife at the company picnic, even if she seems game for it and you *know* you could take her.) But that's more like having a little slider scale on your personality and the sense to know when to dial it up or down as needed as opposed to throwing a switch between the real you and the "alternate" you.

At the end of the day, the swagger win would be to have our work selves and play selves as closely aligned as possible—to achieve the "what you see is what you get" status. If we can knock down this force field that separates us from the world, we can really be seen for who we are and what we bring to the party. Even better, then when our world celebrates us, it's really *us* getting the props, not our bullshit avatars! Step one in filling up that core of you we talked about earlier.

One of my favorite persona-busting moments happened with Andy, and I totally didn't see it coming. I met Andy at the beginning of a three-part series of communication skills workshops for a large conservative organization. He was relatively young, buttoned-down, and new to a senior leadership role. As usual, I kicked off with a discussion about how important it is to fly your 100% unique freak flag. Andy wasn't buying. He argued fiercely on the merits of separating the "work you" from the "personal you." He referred to his corporate persona as a "coat he put on every morning," and he was completely comfortable with this idea.

Naturally, I countered, arguing that this coat of persona was designed to hide who he really was and mask what he was afraid of people seeing. It was a protective mechanism and antithetical to building trust. Back and forth we went.

Then a hand came up from another participant. "Dude," he said to Andy, "when you started working here, I thought you were a bit of an asshole, and I wasn't the only one. It was only after I made the effort to get to know you better, hang out after work and go for beers and stuff, that I realized you were a good guy. But at work? Not so much."

Apparently, that coat wasn't fitting Andy particularly well. He said nothing.

At the second workshop, the same coat-wearing Andy showed up. When he got up to do his speaking bit, I could see his nerves despite the steely effort he was making to try and hide them. He avoided eye contact, paced, and was lacking in any real personality. Despite his efforts to hide his discomfort, my antennae could sense the insecurity coming off him in radiant waves. Suddenly, I had a little *aha*.

I asked Andy if he originally came from a small town. He nodded. *Aha* confirmed.

"Is your family still there?"

Another nod.

"Are you the only one who left and became really successful?"

Andy looked at me sideways and nodded again.

"That's a lot of pressure."

I knew then exactly what was going on with him. Andy still felt like the small-town guy who didn't really merit this fancy-shmancy role in this fancy-shmancy corporation. In his heart of hearts, he didn't believe his true self was worthy of the credibility he'd earned. So, coat on, shield up, game face, and deflect. Persona 10. Swagger 0.

I gently questioned and poked, but Andy was staunch. We opened up the room to a rousing debate about the role of authenticity in leadership. Everyone except Andy agreed that the best leaders expose their vulnerability to their people, and that made them better, more human. In addition, their teams trusted them much more.

The third workshop came several weeks later, and Andy showed up as usual. Shirt, jacket, tie. But his smile was a little looser this time, his eyes less tinged by fear. He laughed more, played more. And when he got up to make his final presentation, things really took a turn.

Before he took the floor, Andy shrugged off his jacket and left it on his chair. This time as he started presenting what he'd learned from the workshops, he kept his eyes firmly on us, scanning and connecting. I watched him intently. Something had changed.

As Andy shared his big takeaways from the program, he loosened his tie and unbuttoned his shirtsleeves—first one, then the other. Then he started to roll them up. As he did, I could see a riot of color emerging from the top of his wrist, then forearm. Andy kept rolling, up to his biceps, and revealed two of the most incredible tattooed sleeves I've ever seen, densely designed from wrist to, I imagine, shoulder. As he exposed his arms, he talked about what he'd learned in the workshops about honesty, vulnerability, and authenticity. He also admitted that since joining the company, he'd never revealed his arms to anyone, even in the summer. Now there he stood, the real, indelible Andy, finally on display for everyone to see.

Of course, I burst into tears. It was one of the most badass displays of swagger I had ever witnessed. And for Andy, it was something he knew he could never go back from.

Swagger for the win. Persona no longer necessary.

I have countless stories like these, and they all end the same way—with someone realizing that they are a complete package, not a mere sum of flawed parts that need to be hidden from the world. Persona is a burden, a heavy coat that we all deserve to throw off so we can experience the giddy bounce and lightness that comes with it.

LOSE THE FALSE FRONT TO REVEAL YOUR REAL SELF

Anyone can learn to confidently nuance words and actions without slipping into a false persona. Here are a few little tricks that can up your game without ever requiring you to fake it.

- **Reclaim your voice.** Stop speaking like every other corporate zombie! Language is such a powerful connector and an incredible tool for deeper connection, curiosity, and acceptance. Start using your own voice to communicate—complete with euphemisms, colloquialisms, and your own culturally rooted slang. Use humor; be playfully smart, and smartly playful. Analogies, metaphors, stories, and real-life examples will all help you to connect in more authentic and memorable ways. Even the occasional expletive can be an incredible equalizer and boundary-breaker. Most of us do it outside of work but are afraid to within corporate walls. If it's natural for you, use it—just not at people. (More on that later.) All of this ladders up to projecting the brand of "you" that no one else could ever replicate!

- **Write like you talk.** See above. Once you learn to start speaking like a human being, start writing like one. Go back to the last ten internal emails you wrote and count the number of buzzwords and acronyms. Now rewrite them using none at all. Do several drafts, imagining different audiences—your sibling, parent, best friend. Can you make yourself understood using plain-speak? Does your personality come out? If you can align the way you talk with the way you write, not only will you start to cement the real you in the minds of your colleagues, but they'll also want to read your emails more!

- **Fly your freak flag high.** We all have weird and wonderful quirks, oddities, or differentiators. Instead of trying to hide them, use them. Maybe you have an accent, a bit of a stutter, a wild way of using your hands when you talk. Don't lose them, use them. This is you. Not only will people remember you more, but also, once you embrace your uniqueness, you'll lose the self-consciousness you've developed around your differences, which in turn will up your confidence. Remember, swagger isn't perfect. It's real.

- **Be vulnerable on purpose.** This strategy applies to people at all levels in the corporate world. If you're a leader, tell your people what scares you and times when you've failed big-time. Show them when you're emotional and share your passion. Doing this proves to them that your persona and humanity are aligned. Let them see you and they will love you for it. And if you're less senior, the same rules apply. Tell your boss what scares you; express your passion or trepidations; tell real-life stories that prove your humanity; empathize with your colleagues when they're hurting. The more human you reveal yourself to be, the more people will be drawn to you. Fact.

- **Be physically casual.** Having an office chat with someone? Perch your ass on a desk or lean against a wall or doorjamb if that's how you feel most comfortable. Don't be afraid to touch someone (appropriately) during a conversation—be it a high five, fist bump, or an encouraging tap on the arm. Ending a meaningful exchange with a peer? If you're a hugger, ask if you can hug them. When we break down some of these physical barriers with pure intent, we close the gap between the work world and the real world. But tread carefully with this one. Your "appropriate" may be someone else's "inappropriate." Err on the side of caution but don't assume it's verboten. If there's any doubt, just ask. "Would you mind if I gave you a serious high five right now, because what you just said was freakin' awesome!"

- **Own your shit.** When you get the opportunity to present to people, own it. Always, always stand. It may seem weird or awkward at first, but it allows you to have a more commanding presence. When you stand in front of a room, you're already telegraphing your power, which then allows you to be more casual and playful. So never be afraid to eat up the space in the room. Instead of overloading slides with info, force the audience to rely on your expertise. You be the info. This way you'll genuinely gain credibility instead of having to fake it. Make serious eye contact at all times. If you're nervous, admit it. Tell the audience why it's important for you to get it right. They'll love you for it. Be seen and let them see you. These are the moments when you get to prove that you have the goods!

- **Consider your style.** Take a look at your wardrobe. Is there a huge discrepancy between your work and play styles? If so, challenge yourself to bring some of your personal flair to your wardrobe. Weekend badass? Forget the dress pants and instead rock some leather action! Wearing the same old suit day after day? Go get a couple of funky shirts and then shrug off that jacket. How we dress is so much a part of who we are, and when we feel both sharply dressed and comfortably us, we feel more powerful.

- **Test perceptions.** Create a little quiz about how you think you're perceived. For example: "Would you consider me playful? Am I someone who likes to take risks? Do you think I'm guarded or more open? What are some of the 'weird' or 'quirky' things you like about me?" Make the questions about things that are important to you. Then ask a few different people to complete the quiz for you—some who know you well personally and others who know you purely professionally. Ask them to be honest. Compare responses. This can be a great reality check on how your authenticity may or may not be coming across and whether your swagger is beginning to manifest. Then work on being more transparent around the things you want people to see, feel, and know about you, and start embracing the stuff that makes you "you" so you can become the best, most authentic version of yourself.

Making it through this exterior persona layer will take practice and courage, but once your real face hits sunlight, you won't ever want to go back and hide in the darkness.

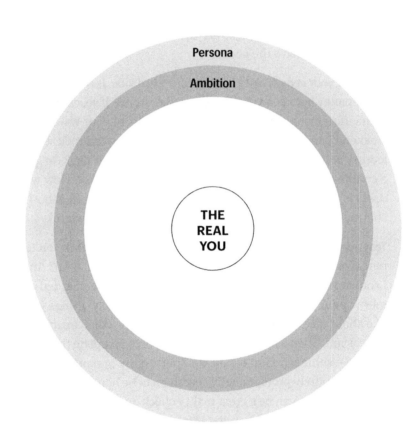

6

AMBITION

OUR NEXT SWAGGER blocker contributes directly to keeping the need for persona alive. It's the nefarious *Ambition*.

Don't get me wrong—I'm all for ambition. In and of itself, it's not a bad thing. But there's a big difference between being purely ambitious and being in your place of excellence. Raw ambition forces you to constantly look skyward, focusing on the next rung up the ladder instead of inward and being present in your journey toward accomplishment on your own terms. Even worse, ambition can cause you to forget to look back at your followers, which will make you a decidedly crappy leader. Ironically, it's the focus on being present and the attention to your people that will help you achieve your goals in the end. Great leaders *need* followers who trust and believe them, and if they do, they will lift you to where you deserve to be. All of this comes by focusing on being in your place of excellence. This requires you to trust yourself and your innate ability to shine. Sounds easy, right?

Not so fast.

In the business world, the concept of ambition is extremely loaded, which is exactly why it qualifies as a swagger blocker. On one end of the ambition spectrum, people who seem comfortable where they are and have no desire to climb the ladder can be accused of being "complacent," of "settling," or being just plain "unambitious"—all of which are unflattering terms. On the other end, those who are perceived as overly ambitious—"driven" or "climbers"—can garner even worse reviews. It's worth noting that this conundrum is even worse for women!

SEEING THROUGH BLIND AMBITION

It's no wonder that swagger can't get past this barrier. It seems you're screwed if you do and screwed if you don't. And it's no coincidence that ambition is sandwiched directly between persona and insecurity. In my experience, together they form the Mighty Triumvirate of Assholeness. We've all seen it: the person who needs to be validated due to massive insecurity, so they wear their title or position like a crown and walk around lopping people's heads off because they believe it's the only way to maintain or grow their power. (*Shudder*.) And we've also seen, or been, the one who has no clue as to why they want to get to the next level or even if it will be a good move but go for it anyway. The world has conditioned us to believe that if power is available to us, we should grab it. Life is better for the powerful, no?

Aligning swagger with ambition is a tricky one. It's human nature to believe that if we want to bark with the big dogs, we need to come across as big dogs ourselves (or, at least, big dogs in training). Otherwise, how will we ever be seen as worthy of a proverbial seat at the table? But that requires us to go to the "fake it 'til you make it" place because we're not yet big dogs, and by definition, until we've actually done the job at the next level up, we technically haven't proved that we're qualified for it. Every time we're promoted, there has to be a leap of faith both by us and the hirer or promoter.

Do you want to get to the next level by being a great faker or by being really freakin' good at the role you're currently in and ready for opportunities to grow that excellence? If your answer is "it depends," I'd argue that you're stuck in ambition. If you're willing to pretend to be anything other than who you really are in order to get to the next level, that says you're ignoring the essence of what swagger is.

This can apply equally if you're working in an organization or as an entrepreneur. In order to be seen as legit, we aggrandize ourselves, claiming more experience or credibility than we actually have because we believe that if we don't, people won't take us seriously. And how can we get the clients if we don't appear to already have an awesome client list, right? That conundrum can swiftly kick us *out of* the very place of excellence that drove our independence to start with and *into* a dangerous, bullshit-filled place that will likely bite us in the ass.

There's a big difference between being purely ambitious and being in your place of excellence.

Remember, swagger requires you to be unchanged by the environment or situation. This doesn't mean you'd show up for an interview or client meeting in your favorite sweatpants (even if they bring you good luck), but it does mean that you don't go into the same situation barking like the big dog you aren't yet.

When we want something very badly, we tend to do whatever we believe it will take to get it. That usually means we'll revert to something that has worked in the past because it's been tested and proved effective. But that doesn't mean it's the right thing to do moving forward. Swagger-fueled ambition requires you to have courage and step into the unknown. You'll need to take chances, be messy, and test your self-belief in order to carve your own unique and well-deserved path to success.

TRUSTING SWAGGER WHEN THE STAKES ARE HIGH

Manny is a perfect example of the kind of courage required to hold on to swagger when the stakes are sky-high. He was a tall, accomplished, good-looking, physically imposing guy with a huge heart, big brain, and puppy-like energy. We met during one of my extended leadership courses. Manny's challenge was that he'd spent years viewing himself through the lens of others. As a result, status, title, and the perception of power had become very important to him, and he'd lost sight of his true value and excellence. Even though he wasn't the kind of guy who would consciously lord power over others, he needed power to make himself feel safe. It's no surprise that he was driven by ambition. In his mind, the bigger the title, the greater the security.

It also makes sense that when his insecurity was triggered, his reaction could be extreme. When he felt out of control or on his back foot, he overcompensated—puffed himself up like a blowfish, then steamrolled through the situation. As a result, when he needed his calm center the most, his good heart and intention would get lost in what came across as in-your-face overassertiveness. Being in his place of excellence went out the window. All he wanted to do was regain status. Not a good look.

We were working on "swagger over status" when an opportunity for a promotion came up within his organization. To up the ante, it was in an area in which Manny had absolutely no experience. But he wanted it badly—not just for the title but for the challenge. I encouraged him to go for it, if for no other reason than to reassess the way he approached the kinds of situations that would historically bring out the absolute worst in him. So, he threw his hat into the ring.

A few weeks later, he got an interview. Cue insecurity and roll out the urge to overcompensate and fake his way to success.

Our session before the interview was akin to a grizzled football coach sending a pumped-up rookie onto the field. Manny was in a lather, itching to get into the game and go for a touchdown.

I gently tugged on his jersey. "OK, dude, you're going to want to impress them with everything you know, show off what a badass you are, blow their minds with your awesomeness. But here's what I want you to do. Resist. Do the opposite. Start by admitting every-thing you *don't* know about the role and why that's exciting and challenging for you. Tell the truth about why you want it. Share your intentions should you get the role. Ask lots of questions and then really listen to their answers. But do not, for one moment, pretend to know more than you do. Forget your ambition. Focus on aspiring to being in your place of excellence. Let them see *you*."

To his credit, and despite fearing that he could blow his biggest career opportunity, he listened.

The day after the interview, Manny reported that for the first time in his career, he had felt 100% like himself in an interview, which had been exhilarating and terrifying in equal measure. What blew his mind was that despite admitting that he didn't have all the answers, they seemed to really like and appreciate him. (Ya think? Insert my eye roll here.)

"You're going to get another interview," I told him. I had zero doubt.

A week later, he was invited for the next round, this time with two VPs from the division he would be working in. He was vibrating with trepidation and excitement as he shared the news.

My coach hat went back on. Now he was potentially facing a power play. Ambition threatened to trump authenticity.

"Hold the line," I told him. "I know that you're going to want to impress them. But remember your swagger. If you hide behind some bullshit corporate persona for the sake of ambition, they will not be able to see you. *Hold the line*." We high-fived, and back into the game he went.

Manny made it through two more rounds of interviews. Despite my wanting to kill any organization that required that many interviews to decide, I was rooting for him hard.

It came down to him and one other candidate. The final hurdle was an "informal chat" with the big "C" to whom everyone reported. We both knew this was make or break time. I had one final affirmation to offer, but it was a doozy. I told him, "If you maintain your swagger, should you get this role, you will *never* have to pretend to be anyone other than exactly who you are. They will be choosing the real you. And if you don't get it, you've just dodged the bullet of bullshit for years to come. Hold the freakin' line!"

Two weeks later, I got an email from Manny.

Subject: I GOT IT

I just found out. I got the new role. Thank you *so much for all your support and encouragement. You have no idea how impactful you have been. You took a big pile of scared mush and turned it into me . . . I can't help but get emotional thinking about all the love and support that you sent my way every time you gave me the "talks" . . .*

I share this not to blow smoke up my own ass (although getting love and kudos is always super-appreciated); instead, it's to contextualize a key phrase: "You took a big pile of scared mush and turned it into me." Manny had learned that his ambition had been driven by insecurity and fear—and that's exactly what had been holding him back. Not his competency, not his potential, not his status. He'd never been able to believe that he could accomplish his goals just by being himself. But this situation had proved it once and for all. Imagine how that would change his journey and his approach to leadership moving forward!

SWAGGER WILL NEVER HOLD YOU BACK FROM SUCCESS

The way you perceive ambition will impact your swagger on a daily basis—not just when the stakes are super-high, as in an interview situation. Instead of constantly looking skyward for the next great opportunity or senior ass-kissing position, you want to align ambition and swagger, which means you spend your time looking inward to better understand yourself and, more importantly, focus on the people who rely on you for support and leadership. Just because you're not walking around carrying a ladder does not mean you're unambitious. It simply means you have the confidence to believe that when the opportunities present themselves, you'll be ready to take them on without having to change a thing about who you are.

The *Oxford English Dictionary*'s definition of ambition is "a strong desire to do or to achieve something, typically requiring determination and hard work." It's not about a title or power. It's wanting to be a badass to the best of your ability and for the right reasons. For ambition to be legit, it should *never* come at the cost of your authenticity. That's too big of a trade-off. Being perfect is not the gateway to accomplishment; being human is.

For ambition to be legit, it should never come at the cost of your authenticity.

I know, I know: some of you are reading this and thinking, "Riiight, like I'm going to achieve my goals by revealing that I'm a mere messy mortal." But try to step back from your insecurities for a second and think about it logically. Who do you trust more out in the real world: someone who appears to be perfect or someone with whom you can connect on a human level? Both people require your approval in order to achieve their goals. But if you smell bullshit or feel they're pushing for something, are you more likely to accept or resist? If they tell you stories about how they overcame obstacles, share something they're still aspiring to, or let you in on their humanity, are you more likely to take a chance on them or pass?

Morgan faced this very challenge in her male-dominated corporate world. A small, blond, whip-smart woman, she joined the bank at twenty-two. It took her all of five minutes to decide that the best way to succeed was to fit the mold of the men around her. "There was a look, mannerisms, a package I felt I had to be," she says. "There was a way to articulate your ideas, words to use if you were angry or happy. It was all very scripted. I thought I had to follow it because I was so much younger than everyone else. The only thing I revealed to people was stuff I couldn't change—my gender, age, height, the color of my skin. On the authenticity scale, I was about a 5."

But Morgan had big plans. "I was about a 30 out of 10 on the ambition scale," she admits. "I was completely focused on looking for the next big role and taking over the world."

When I introduced Morgan to the concept of swagger, she was already well on her way up the ladder. At twenty-six, she was one of the youngest senior managers in the place and had her eye firmly on an associate VP title before she hit thirty. So when she heard that she might be able to better achieve her goals by dropping her guard, exposing her humanity, and revealing herself as imperfect, she was totally skeptical. "I thought, 'Wow, this is a great way to make me look stupid, and I'm not for that,'" she says. "I wanted to stand out, but sure as hell not for looking bad." But she stuck with the training, admittedly resisting all the way.

Success comes when you're able to be real.

—MORGAN

What she didn't realize was that the desire for swagger has a way of infiltrating your psyche. You start to imagine how good it might feel if you *could* be yourself, speak your truth, and drop your guard. The beneficial "what ifs" begin creeping in, and once they do, swagger starts to bubble up.

The effects were subtle at first. She started getting positive comments on the very things she'd been insecure about. "Suddenly, I was being told I was wise beyond my years instead of just 'young.'" The next *aha* came when she met with a peer she hadn't seen in months. "Within a half hour, he was like, 'You're a lot more open than you used to be,'" she says. "I was surprised because it wasn't something I was conscious of. He said, 'It's the way you're talking about a challenge you had. You never used to admit that you *have* challenges!' I realized that now I hadn't been afraid to be real with him."

The big proof came when Morgan was offered the role she'd been dreaming of. At twenty-eight, she made associate vice president—

virtually unheard of in that organization until that point. The catch was that her predecessor had retired out of the job, which he'd held forever, and most of his team had been with the bank longer than Morgan had been alive!

The time came for her to address the entire division at an event. "I was coming in as their new leader, and as a new executive on top of that, which was incredibly uncomfortable for me," she says. "I realized that I needed to make a genuine connection with these people quickly because doing my usual shtick of 'I'm really qualified' wasn't going to resonate with them. That was when I knew I'd have to tap into what I'm most uncomfortable with—being vulnerable and more authentic. I needed to tap into my swagger so badly to show them who I was and what I saw for all of us. But it was in direct opposition to what I'd always believed leaders should be—polished and perfect."

Morgan chose swagger over ambition and let the team see the real her in her true place of excellence. The results were even better than she'd imagined. Not only did this new team accept her as their leader, but they were also able to embrace who she really was.

"I'm not afraid to use 'millennial-speak,' even though they tease me about it," Morgan says. "I've embraced a style of communicating, dressing, and interacting with people at work that is just authentic and normal. What I see now is that I'm modeling this for the rest of my team and proving that this is a place where they can embrace their own swagger. On top of that, the amount of energy I used to spend trying to be someone else has been freed up for things that really matter, like driving better collaboration or building a better organization. You can get so caught up in the distraction of ambition and persona that you forget that at the end of the day, it just doesn't matter. You're a far better human when you're just keeping it real, and that's good for everyone."

Over the last few years, Morgan's success has continued to grow, but on her terms. "If you think of any inspirational leader," she says, "it's not the phony business muppets that people want to get behind. It's the people who have figured out how to master true swagger.

Sure, it's uncomfortable to get there, but that's part of the journey. I can attest to the fact that success comes when you're able to be real."

EMBRACE SWAGGER AND ASCEND YOUR UNIQUE LADDER

The road to swagger in the face of ambition can be a particularly rocky one. There will be bumps, detours, and setbacks. But having a strong sense of your value, knowing exactly where you are in your journey (and why that's OK), and understanding the benefits of being your authentic self can work wonders.

Answering these questions can provide clarity on how and why you might be stuck in the ambition zone and, more importantly, how to use your authentic self as a superpower to get where you want to be. (*Psst! These questions can be an incredibly helpful tool if and when you're preparing for an interview or work review situation.*)

1   What is your place of excellence? List all of the things you know you're very good at in the workplace.

2   What are the things you're still working on that you hope to be great at eventually?

3   Why are you a valuable asset to any team?

4   What makes you different, unique, weird, funky, or freaky in comparison to your peers? List everything, not just what you think is "good" or acceptable.

5   How might these differentiators be assets to your organization? (For example, you might have a different country of origin from others at work, which makes you self-conscious. But the assets can be everything from making you more empathetic to others' journeys, to speaking multiple languages, to bringing diversity and diversity of thought to the team.)

6 What do you wish people at work knew about you that would give you more freedom to be your true self?

7 List three ways you could show that hidden quality to people, and to whom, specifically, you would reveal it.

8 List five things you believe are stopping you from achieving your goals at work.

9 List five things you believe you could better accomplish if you had swagger at work.

10 Imagine you have achieved your goals. Now consider: What do you want to be known for or as?

Don't let your ambition blind you or block your swagger. The best way to find the ladder that's the result of your great work and greater humanity is to keep your eyes and heart wide open. Then watch as the world lifts you one rung at a time. Swagger on up, people. The world is waiting for your awesomeness.

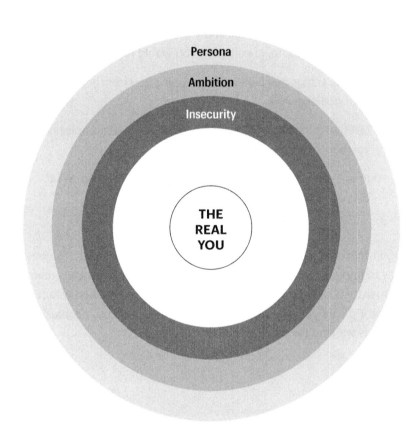

7

INSECURITY

THE NEXT SWAGGER blocker is a doozy. It pretends to validate ambition and reinforces the need for persona via that little voice in your head that says, "Maybe you should play it safe and just agree with whatever the boss says. And for goddess' sake, do not show weakness! No one will ever give you opportunities if they see the cracks in your armor. If you want to make it around here, you'd better play the game."

This bullshit comes to us courtesy of *Insecurity*.

Insecurity is the dreaded "what if"—the anxious state where all unknowns percolate. It's self-doubt in action. And in the business world, there will *always* be people who will happily validate it for you. Walking into every presentation or meeting worrying about whether your message will resonate is like wearing a "kick me" sign. Guaranteed, you'll get a kick in the ass from someone who's even more insecure than you are. No better way for the haters to build themselves up than by kicking you down—a classic bullying move.

The corporate world feeds on insecurity, using it as a negative force to get ever more out of us. If we're always freaked out that someone might be judging our worth or questioning us, we'll amp up our game, right? Wrong. Insecurity is spirit-sucking, and it doesn't help us manifest our best selves. Even if our swagger manages to permeate outward, without quieting the defeatist voices in our heads, it's likely to get stopped in its tracks by the insecurity blocker.

Even those of us who consider ourselves relatively confident can get sidelined by insecurity and turn into permission-seeking grovelers or, worse, pot-shot takers who try to distract from our own issues by momentarily highlighting someone else's.

Insecurity is pervasive, corrosive, and one nasty beast to tame. Everyone has it, even Barack Obama, Oprah Winfrey, and Elon Musk. Sure, it's natural to second-guess yourself. At times, it can even be a useful tool to double check whether you're prepared or not. But when insecurity becomes self-limiting, it's harmful.

SIFTING THROUGH INSECURITY TO FIND REALITY

There's a big difference between being concerned about taking risks (which can understandably throw you off your center a little) and worrying about whether you'll get called out for not knowing what you're talking about. Let's break it down. If you're standing in front of a room sharing your expertise or perspective, there's a reason you're there. If you truly *don't* have anything of value to offer, you should probably sit the hell down until you do. But let's assume you're at the meeting or event because someone in their infinite wisdom decided you were the right person to represent. That's because you had some swagger in the first place. Never forget that.

Here's something I've learned about the dynamics of being asked to step into the spotlight at work. It's never just your reputation on the line. Your boss will be hoping you don't make them look bad. Your peers will be expecting you to showcase the project or team in a positive way. And anyone else who contributed to your knowledge will be hoping you can add some value. No pressure! But if you are so poorly equipped to pay off these ridiculously high expectations, then why were you chosen in the first place? Would anyone ask you to stand there if they knew you'd fall apart? Does anyone want to take credit for that person who got up in front of the room and literally peed in their pants? Not in my experience. (Although it does make for good urban legend.)

Remember that those voices in your head do not suddenly manifest—they've been simmering and solidifying for years, seeded by your parents, siblings, teachers, boyfriends and girlfriends, colleagues, and bosses your entire life. When someone tells us we're not good enough, it sticks. Those tapes get recorded and then play themselves over and over when we're at our most vulnerable. Every recording begins with "What if…" and ends with some imagined disaster. It's rarely about the challenge we're about to take on—rather, it's the history around the self-doubt that is the killer. That mindset gets so entrenched that even when we're celebrated or have a major irrefutable success, the positive message has to work itself through all of the layers we talked about in order to even begin to have an impact on our self-perception.

Insecurity is rarely about the challenge we're about to take on—it's the history of self-doubt that is the killer.

Add to that the fact that our brains are actually wired to need absolute certainty. A team of researchers at the UCL Institute of Neurology devoted an entire study to proving how freakin' stressful "not knowing for sure" actually is.[6] What they discovered is that we crave knowing the outcome of a stressful situation so much that even in a fifty-fifty situation, our brains will automatically go to the negative first and assume the worst just to put ourselves out of the misery of the "what if."

This science played out in the real world explains why we'd rather accept we're going to suck than hope we don't. This also reinforces Imposter Syndrome. Our brain's warped logic tells us that if we accept and prepare ourselves to be told we're full of shit, then we don't have to worry about it anymore. Cue the never-ending loop of insecurity.

How messed up is that?

TURNING THE "WHAT IFS" INTO "WHAT IF NOTS"

Do not think for a second that I'm a stranger to insecurity. I've had thousands of moments, and I've learned from every single one.

One of the greatest lessons came when I was living in the UK and my agent got me an audition for a new TV show called *The Fashion Police*. Not the bitchy red-carpet critique version, but a kinder, gentler precursor that was about giving people surprise makeovers and celebrating local designers from across the country. I was twenty-eight years old and already had one failed TV show to my non-famous name. To say my self-esteem wasn't exactly romping through fields of daisies would be fair. And then there was the worry that my agent was going to drop me if I didn't nail a gig soon. My terror about my prospects was singing a death dirge in my ear. I remember feeling like utter crap. I had everything to lose and everything to gain. Fifty-fifty, baby.

The audition went like this. I was invited to Anglia Studios in front of a midsize audience. They had just been a part of a Phil Donahue– style interview show about the aftermath of the murder of a local teen—and now they were going to see *my audition*. I shit you not!

The Fashion Police showrunner briefed me. "OK, just go out there and talk fashion with them. Have some fun. Get them excited! Lots of energy now," and she gave me a little shove. I stumbled onto the studio floor. My mind went blank. The audience watched me expectantly. I felt frozen. This paralysis probably lasted only seconds, but to me, it was eons. I had no idea what to do. What the hell was I going to say to these people about fashion to make them forget that minutes ago they'd been talking about *murder*?

And then I saw him. In the front row sat a monk, dressed in a frock that looked kinda like a stiff brown nightgown. If I couldn't use him as comedy fodder, then I deserved to have my TV host license revoked.

"We all wear uniforms to define who we are," I started. "Some wear suits and ties, some wear jeans and tees, and some wear nightgowns." I gestured at the monk. The crowd giggled nervously. "But it's often what we can't see that makes us interesting. What's underneath the uniform reveals so much about who we really are. Sir," I beckoned to my frocked friend, "would you join me up here?" He smiled warmly and came to stand next to me.

This was the moment. Fifty-fifty. Do or die. All in.

"May I ask what kind of underwear you have on?" I asked the monk. The room exploded in laughter.

For the next fifteen minutes, I talked undies. Boxers versus briefs, thongs versus granny panties, sexy versus serviceable. My new side-kick became my straight man as I poked and prodded members of the audience to reveal their philosophies and fashion choices around lingerie. The crowd warmed, showing bra straps, admitting peccadilloes, debating merits as they ate up the time like candy.

The showrunner was snort-laughing, her hand clamped over her mouth. She gave me the "two minutes left to wrap up" signal.

I went in for the kill. I turned to this lovely and generous man who had accepted my teasing so gracefully and said, "OK... after all of this, we're dying to see for ourselves. Sir, will you reveal your underpants?" Half of the room died of laughter and the other half nearly died. Without batting an eyelash, he lifted his frock past his gartered socks, over his knobby knees, to display a graying pair of tighty-whiteys. The audience cheered, and he dropped his frock with a grin.

And then it was over. I started to shake again. Had I gone too far? Had I insulted someone's religion? Had I blown my shot? The showrunner came over, shook my hand, and told me they'd be in touch.

I went home, drank wine, and waited. And waited.

About a week later, my agent called. "You got it," he told me simply.

I yelped.

"And you also got another show."

"*What*??" I asked in disbelief. Little did I know that whenever anyone auditioned at Anglia, they would flip on all of the monitors in the various production offices in the building so that they could watch out for potential talent. One of these teams was looking for a host for another late-night variety show and, after seeing my audition, decided to offer me that gig as well.

Two hosting jobs with one audition. Just when I had thought I was the least equipped, least capable, and least saleable, I killed it. Why? Because I was shit-scared and did it anyway. Unapologetically and all in. Everything to lose and everything to gain. I went from not knowing to proving. But I had to *do* it first.

RETRAINING YOUR INSECURITY BRAIN

Part of battling insecurity is learning to shut it down before it really worms its way in and takes hold, controlling first your thoughts and then your actions.

Has this ever happened to you? You do or say something that makes you feel really badass, and within seconds, your brain is questioning it. The inner monologue goes something like, "Holy shit! I can't believe I just said that. He so deserved it. Claiming that was his idea was such bullshit. Someone needed to say something, so I did. Holy *shit* . . . oh no. What if everyone thinks I'm a pain in the ass or trying to claim credit myself? I'm such an idiot. Why did I even say anything? No one cares about what I think anyway, and now I've just brought attention to myself for something negative. Why do I always do that? I'm *such* an idiot!"

Part of battling insecurity is learning to shut it down before it really worms its way in and takes hold.

Sound familiar? I know it happens to me *all the time*. These insecurity-fueled, self-sabotaging mind-fucks are referred to as Negative Automatic Thoughts, or NATs, as I like to call them. They're like nasty little annoying bugs flitting around in our heads, both irritating and distracting. And they will try to gnaw your swagger moments down to the bone.

NATs are at the heart of insecurity and the result of years of conditioning. They are like a secondary trigger or fuse that sets off a chain reaction designed to keep you paralyzed by self-doubt. The act happens, the brain kicks in with a NAT, the NAT spirals, and before you know it, you're utterly convinced that the situation is in no way the triumph you momentarily imagined it; rather, it's now a disaster of epic proportion. You cannot build swagger on this foundation because the very events designed to fill up and empower the real you instead become something that can trigger a sense of danger or unease. We need to correct that shit ASAP.

Just as in life, everything has its counterbalance. And NATs are no different. Just as there can be an immediate negative thought, there can be an equally powerful positive one, once you learn how to phrase it. Take *that*, NAT.

A Positive Automatic Thought (PAT) is when an initial thought or questioning takes a very different turn. So, if the inner monologue starts with, "Holy shit! I can't believe I just said that" and threatens to begin a downward spiral of self-flagellation, you have the power to change its course. How about this for the continuation: "He so deserved it. Claiming that was his idea was such bullshit. Someone needed to say something so I did. Holy *shit*... I am a warrior! Check me out. I spoke the truth. I was actually brave enough to call someone out. And it doesn't matter what happens. Now people know that I'm brave enough to tell the truth and hopefully they'll trust me more. For the freakin' *win*!"

See? A PAT is a literal pat on the back for the thought, moment, or accomplishment.

It takes mere seconds for a thought to go one way or the other. That's how much time your brain has to make that decision. You have to act immediately. Let me tell you, it is much easier to start with a PAT than it is to turn a NAT into a PAT. And I would argue that we all can all feel a NAT coming—because we know how our minds work. If you're someone who's conditioned to quickly go to the dark side, it's almost as if you're preplanning the script even before it's conscious.

The secret to success is to start preplanning the PAT, even if it just feels like words at first. It might feel like there are dual audio tracks playing in your head. Just remember that one is conditioning, and one is *truth*. We've got to let the truth track play as long and as loud as the NAT track has been playing, until it finally has the potency to drown it out.

**Retrain your brain to accept what is true
instead of what is imagined.**

So, when you have the high of a swagger moment, stop, drop, and listen to what happens in your brain. The second you hear your moment taking a negative turn, grab your NAT by the cojones and give it a squeeze. Own your thoughts and quickly get PAT-ing. Remind yourself that it's just your old, negatively conditioned brain talking. Your heart knows the truth. Rewrite it fast.

Another practical way to unlearn insecurity is by aligning perception with reality—start retraining your brain to accept what is *true* instead of what is imagined. Because what's up in our heads is *always* worse than what really "is." While we can never guarantee the certainty of success, we sure as hell can prove to ourselves the limited likelihood of failure. We can record over those bullshit tapes—daily, progressively, and permanently.

Here's a practical exercise that works wonders.

> Grab a notebook that no one but you will ever see. For the next five high-stakes meetings or presentations you have planned, you're going to use this notebook as a bullshit detector.

Fold a page in half. Write "Perception" on the top of one column and "Reality" on the other. Before your meeting, presentation, or whatever scary thing, write down everything you're insecure about in the Perception column. Get those "what ifs" out of your head and onto the page. Really go wild. No one is going to see this. Vent and spew all concerns, no matter how bizarre or unlikely they may be. "I'm worried that my boss is going to think I'm an idiot"; "I'm afraid I'll have a wardrobe malfunction and flash the room." Anything goes.

Then go into the room and do your thing. Immediately after you're done (the timing of this is important), come back to the book and write down everything that actually happened in the Reality column—bad and good. For example, "My boss threw me a hardball and I knocked it out of the park." Close the book and walk away.

Do this for a minimum of five different events. Don't reread or overthink—just do.

Once you've completed the exercise, grab a highlighter and go back to the first page. Highlight everything that was duplicated in both columns—meaning that you imagined it and then it actually occurred. If you were worried you'd pass out and require CPR and it actually happened—highlight away. If not, move on to the next item. Do that for all five pages.

Now really look at how many of those insecurities came to fruition. What were you worried about that paid off? Are there tons of highlights? Validation for the insecurities? I guarantee you will be surprised by what you discover.

The last step is to fold all of the pages you wrote on so that only the Reality side is showing.

Anything you've highlighted that was negative, and that you believe is actually within your realm of control to do differently, is now your cheat sheet for what you need to work on improving.

That's what's real. The rest of those insecurities are not real. If you have to repeat this exercise thirty times to prove it, knock yourself out. Until you actively challenge those perceptions, you'll be victim to your tapes.

TAMING THE INSECURITY BEAST

We will all screw up or fall short hundreds of times in our lives—no matter how smart, competent, or badass we are. But if we let those past moments dictate our attitude moving forward, we'll be paralyzed. Having swagger does not mean you'll be immune to self-doubt, but it will sure as hell dictate what to do with that doubt.

Having swagger does not mean you'll be immune to self-doubt, but it will sure as hell dictate what to do with that doubt.

If you're worried that you're not ready, get as ready as you can and then tell people where you are. If you believe you're not capable enough, work to the strengths you do have and ask other people for help in learning to be better. Be where you are and own it! Why is it that your boss seems to have their shit together better than you? If they're worth their salt, it's probably because they've been screwing up and learning from it longer than you have.

Bottom line? Giving in to insecurity keeps you stuck: you can't ask smarter people for help and guidance because you'll have to confess your shortcomings in order to get their input. Wanting to be great is a beautiful and admirable thing. But it requires development, risk-taking, and vulnerability—all key if you want to attain swagger. Let your successes be your proof and your shit-show moments act as learning. You might not know what the outcomes are going to be, but if your swagger stays strong, you'll spend less time worrying about the crap you can't control and more time focusing on the stuff you can.

So to hell with self-doubt. It's a nasty beast that feeds on those ugly (and useless) voices in your head. There's proof that when you tame that beast (and you *can* tame it), your swagger can make that magical romp right through not only insecurity but also ambition and persona.

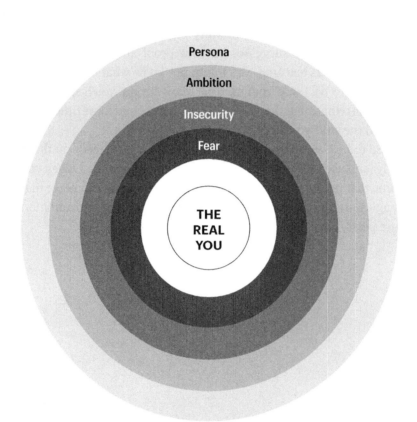

8

FEAR

THE NEXT SWAGGER blocker is one we're all way too familiar with—the literally dreaded *Fear*.

Hooray for fear! It's a sensible preventive measure against doing super-dumb stuff like tickling wild tigers or free-climbing up cliff faces (cuz both are really bad ideas in my book—*and this is my book*). Right?

There's just one teeny-weeny caveat: fear isn't particularly smart. It doesn't have the ability to discern between what might be life-threatening and something unknown whose potential outcome we don't know. Fear is a limiter and paralyzer that will always, always assume the worst, and in doing so, throw gasoline on the fires that help insecurity, ambition, and persona burn bright. It's also where confidence ultimately goes to die a horrible death.

I was in the mountains of Colorado delivering a storytelling experience for Danone North America, a food and beverage company based in Boulder. From the moment I met them, I could tell these were my people. Open, friendly, potty-mouthed, and genuine. Their company culture was laid-back, easygoing, and, well, *real*. They were like the organizational equivalent of a hug. I was having tons of fun helping them gain the confidence they needed to tell the kind of authentic stories they aspired to.

During the break, a woman came up to me and asked for advice. "I'm always so terrified when I have to get up and talk about my work," she confessed. "I just fall apart. I don't know what to do."

**Fear is where confidence goes
to die a horrible death.**

I was taken aback. Despite working in the warmest, fuzziest, and most obviously inclusive corporate culture I'd encountered in a while, here was this poor woman who was still shit-scared of speaking her truth.

I asked her what, specifically, was so scary for her. "I'm not really sure," she said. "Maybe that someone will think I'm not smart."

"Are you smart? Do you know what you're doing?"

She nodded.

"OK, then, anyone who didn't think you were smart would be wrong, yes?"

"Well, yeah," she said. "But they could still think it."

"And then what?" I countered.

We went on to play one of my favorite fear-facing games, "And Then What?" It's pretty simple: all you have to do is follow the scariest version of your worst nightmare situation to its inevitable conclusion, step by step. In my experience, the game usually plays out as follows.

"So I get up in front of the room and start to talk. (And then what?) Then I look at people and I can see they're a bit skeptical. (And then what?) Then I start to get more nervous and my voice shakes a little. (And then what?) And then I start to fumble my words. I forget something important. I have to look at my notes. (And then what?) My boss gives me the stink eye. People start checking their phones. (And then what?) After the presentation, my boss tells me she is disappointed and I need to do better next time. (And then what?)..."

For the sake of brevity, I'll cut to the chase. Most of the time I play this game, the final line is something like, "And then I lose my job, and within two months, I'm homeless on the street."

Seriously. Homeless? On the street? The second the worriers stand up in front of people to share their work, their brains are already cutting to them lying under a bridge in a sleeping bag. No wonder they want to barf!

So I ask them where they think their story starts to become unrealistic. Usually, it's around the "I have to look at my notes" mark. The stink eye from the boss isn't even a real detail. And yet...

YOUR BRAIN IS THE SCARIEST PLACE

I've come to realize that fear has nothing to do with specific corporate culture or situations. For example, people will tell me that they're fine when they have to deal with a small room of, say, three people, but add five more people to the mix and suddenly it's like an episode of *Fear Factor*. Others will say they're cool talking to a room of a thousand, but a presentation to four senior people will have them peeing in their pants. And then there are some who say that they're happy to present to strangers, but having to share their ideas with colleagues and peers has them throwing up in the bathroom.

Here's the reality: Fear isn't triggered by your environment; it's triggered by your brain and its context, or lack of it. Fear is also the greatest swagger-sucker out there.

Why does this happen? Most people who get this scared have been conditioned over time. That time you did a presentation on tree frogs in second grade and didn't realize your fly was down? Check. Playing Dorothy in *The Wizard of Oz* at summer camp and forgetting the words to "Somewhere over the Rainbow"? Oh, yeah. Interviewing for that coveted job and accidentally mentioning the wrong company name? Doing your first big presentation to the chief marketing officer of a global foods company, who when you use the phrase "I think..." interrupts you with, "Young lady, I don't pay for what you think. I pay for what you *know*"? Bingo! (This happened to me.) All of these smallish incidents chip away at your psyche, building up to a collective mental baseline that says, "Getting up in front of people is dangerous." Once that happens, you're in trouble. Because the brain also can't differentiate between "a tiger is going to eat me" fear and "I don't want to look like an idiot" fear.

Now let's add the challenge of being purposefully vulnerable, which means you're more subject to that "danger." Remember, swagger requires you to let down your guard, because if nothing can get in, then nothing can get out. And if your fear is extreme, the amount of energy you'll spend on being stuck between self-protection and openness can be not only exhausting but also terribly confusing for the brain. That means you won't be able to effectively process what's coming at you, be it a hardball question or an encouraging smile. This creates its own perpetual cycle of keeping you paralyzed.

**Swagger requires you to
let down your guard, because if nothing
can get in, then nothing can get out.**

This doesn't just apply to common fears of things like public speaking. The same cycle is triggered whenever you're in an unknown situation that, in your mind, has high stakes. Asking for a raise or promotion, confronting a colleague or a boss, taking on a new project, making a career change—all of these can determine the trajectory of your future. And they all can be determined by your ability and willingness to move past your fear.

Robin, a well-respected advertising professional in her late forties, admits that she's been plagued by fear for much of her career. She became hyperaware of it when she was an up-and-coming account director in her thirties.

"I was pulled into a meeting with my CEO, who wanted to talk to me about a pitch we had lost," she says. "He felt that we didn't win the business because the senior client, a woman, hadn't liked me. He started lecturing me about how I came across in meetings, and said that there was something he just couldn't put his finger on that made me the type of person women responded negatively to. He warned me to be more aware of how I presented myself, how I dressed, talked, and came across in meetings so that 'women in the room don't feel threatened.'

"I was floored," Robin continues. "I didn't think this woman was reacting to just me. She wasn't hitting it off with *anyone* in the room, including the guy beside me. But I was too scared to challenge him. So it stuck with me. And it stayed stuck. I'd always considered myself as having a casual, easygoing style. There was nothing inappropriate about what I wore or how I held myself. In fact, it was probably the very thing that helped me grow my division so successfully. But from then on, fear was always with me. I toned myself down whenever the CEO was present. I made myself smaller to appease him and avoid conflict."

Cut to ten years later. Robin had become the president of an agency in her own right. She'd experienced proof of success year after year, gained a stellar reputation, and was at the top of her game. But still, the fear plagued her. "To people who don't know me, I come across as incredibly confident," she says. "I'm loud. I tell jokes. But the truth is that I deal with insecurity and fear every minute of every day. What people think they see is not the reality. I would say there's 50% of me that fights Imposter Syndrome daily."

So when Robin's CEO, a very well-established ad man and speaker, asked her to step up into the role of CEO so he could focus more on his speaking career, she was hit by a tidal wave of swagger-blocking fear. "I was absolutely terrified," she admits. "I just didn't believe that I fit the mold!" Immediately, she started backpedaling. "I told him that maybe we should wait until I'd grown the agency by another million dollars, so that maybe I'd feel like I deserved it or something. 'That's ridiculous,' he told me. 'You're already running the agency, so you should have the title.' So it was him pushing me to do it and me moving forward with *such* trepidation, I can't even tell you!"

Reluctantly, Robin accepted the role. Even then, she was consumed with fear over what the industry reaction would be. "I have tons of people asking to meet me for coffee. 'I'm interested in your journey,' they say. 'You have such a unique style. I'd like to hear more about how you did it.' But still, only a part of me can accept that I deserve this," she admits. "It's a constant struggle. The perception is that I'm walking around super-confident in my abilities, when the reality is that's only half of the time. The other half, I'm just plain petrified."

The lesson here is that you can be scared shitless and still experience great success. But as Robin will attest to, fear makes the journey that much harder. It also robs you of so much of the joy and self-satisfaction that comes with accomplishment. That's just a part of what you'll lose out on unless you can move your swagger through the fear. If you don't take the time to face it down *every time* it tries to face *you* down, it will build and take hold in ways that could take you a lifetime to shake off.

If Robin, with all of her proof points, hasn't yet been able to fully conquer the monster, you're probably wondering, "what the hell can *I* do about it?"

Fear is real. It doesn't matter what the danger is. Telling someone, or yourself, to "just get over it" doesn't work. So let's get practical. The trick is going to be in building up some positive conditioning to counter the brain's certainty that all is about to go to hell in a hand basket.

DEMYSTIFYING FEAR

Let's start with demystifying what fear actually is and where it comes from. If you bisect the brain, you'll see that it's broken into three major sections. This view is known as the triune brain. At the base of the brain, there's the brain stem, or, the reptilian brain. Back when we were little tadpoles in the primordial evolutionary sludge, this was all we had to work with. This part of the brain is responsible for all of our fear, anger, and basic survival instincts such as food and sex; fight, flight, and freeze. Without this part, we never would have evolved into the gloriously complex beings we are now. But back in the day, we were a reactionary shit show. This lizard brain has no ability to reason. It can only respond to what's in front of it. If it's scary, kill it, run like hell, or stand frozen like a deer in headlights. But without it, we never would have been able to survive, thrive, and evolve—which led to the development of the limbic system.

**If you don't face fear down every time
it tries to face you down, it will build and take hold
in ways that could take a lifetime to shake off.**

The limbic, or mammalian, brain houses all of our emotions. It's capable of memory, selective response, judgment, and all kinds of other juicy subconscious stuff that makes us human. When we react to fear, this part of the brain stores the memory of it. Unfortunately, there's also no real reasoning in this section, so if events are scary or traumatic enough, the limbic brain will hang on to the remnants for eons. *Ouch.*

Above all of this is the neocortex, the newest part of the brain and the big processor of information. This is where all of our complex human thinking lives: reasoning, creativity, problem solving—all the stuff that fundamentally separates us from animals. Trouble is, unlike the reptilian and limbic systems, this part of the brain needs to be consciously activated. If we can't take a step back from our emotional and fearful responses, we're stuck in an endless behavioral loop.

To make this even tougher, there's a little switch called the amygdala that sits at the juncture of the reptilian and limbic brains, which, when triggered by fear or uncertainty, squirts cortisol, the stress hormone, into the system. This causes major system freak-out and shutdown. Adrenaline floods the body to prepare for the battle royale it assumes is about go down. And to make absolutely sure that no rational thought gets in the way of a win, the neocortex gets switched off. All your brain wants you to do in the face of danger is make you *run, you idiot*; *kill it, dummy*; or *do not move*. Subtle, huh?

OK, so now you have a visual on all of this action. But how does this all impact us when we're at work? Surely we can't perceive the danger to be that serious—can we?

Hell to the yeah, we can. The reptilian brain is constantly seeking a host of base desires like dominance, power, positive self-image, and submission in others. Now imagine all of that in a boardroom situation. If the lizard brain feels threatened by posturing, power dynamics, or scrutiny, it's going to want to have a cage match. Adrenaline goes to work and our bodies start to freak out with the shakes, shallow breathing, blotchy redness, paralysis, and, my favorite, sparkle brain. That's when you go to reach for information from the neocortex only to discover that as a result of the fear trigger, the drawbridge has been raised and all useful words and thinking have been cut off. *Run, you idiot.* Oy vey. Oh, and then the limbic brain stores the entire experience in a useful little video playback system so you can relive the horror over and over again. This is how negative programming happens, and yet another reason why swagger and its required vulnerability are so freakin' hard to accomplish. Your conscious brain is telling you that being open and accessible is a great idea, while your unconscious mind is chanting "sucker, sucker, sucker."

Now you know why whenever you have to do a presentation, be part of a high-stakes meeting, or face a one-on-one with someone "superior," and be your authentic and vulnerable self, you lose your ever-lovin' mind—even if you're at an open and positive company. It isn't your fault: it's your brain reliving every negative experience you've ever had to ensure you don't just keep your status intact, but also emerge victorious . . . and alive.

But there are ways to outsmart the nefarious triune brain system.

FACING DOWN THE FEAR FACTOR

First thing: don't try doing it when you're already shit-scared. Utterly useless. If you're not in your right mind, nothing will stick. And you're going to need your limbic and neocortex systems for this one. So make sure you have access to them. Pick a time when you have nothing high stakes at play. Because we're about to make a plan that will retrain your brain. What we're going to do is start to shift what your triggers are, because if your brain can't find the obviously fearful element in a situation, it won't begin the negative downward spiral.

Start by making a list of everything you can remember scarring you at work. That time your boss called you out in front of a packed boardroom? Write down what happened. When you blanked out during a presentation and stood gaping like a fish for what felt like an eternity? Jot it down. Let's not forget the time you were dissing a colleague in the bathroom only to discover she was in one of the stalls the whole time. Shame on you—but capture it anyway.

Now we're going to pretend that these scenarios haven't happened yet. Instead, we're going to plan for the possibility. For each scenario, write down five possible ways to not just handle the situation, but also turn it to your advantage. Write the steps, script, and desired outcomes.

For example: *My boss could publicly call me out for not being prepared enough for a presentation.* Here is a list of possible options.

1 Make sure I run my overview past the boss in advance. Get their buy-in and ask for a little bit of their input. Then quote them during the presentation and credit them for being insightful so they look good. Score!

2 Start the presentation by clearly articulating what the ask was so people understand my area of focus. Then if anyone calls me out, I can explain why it wasn't covered. This way I'll narrow the possibilities of actually missing something, or at least the perception of it.

3 Run the top-line content past three different colleagues before building the presentation. Take their input and credit them with helping at the start of the presentation. This way, I'll gain their support during the presentation and won't get singled out.

4 Go to my boss in advance and straight-up confess that getting called out in front of people is my biggest fear. Tell them what a good job I want to do and ask for their mentorship. Turn my boss into an empathetic supporter who would look like an asshole for doing anything other than helping me succeed.

5 In the moment, rely on my truth, intention, and self-belief. If I get called out, apologize for having disappointed them. Express what my intention was for the presentation and let them know that I'm capable of achieving my goals. Ask for their immediate feedback on how I could improve, so they put their money where their mouth is.

See how this can neatly shut down the "And Then What?" game? The more you plan, the more your neocortex will remain in the driver's seat. Now, if any of these scenarios play out, you'll have conscious steps to mitigate or interrupt perceived threats to your power, dominance, and self-image. Of course, you can document your results for proof of which concepts work best in what scenarios. No more fear of the unknown, no more pure stress response, no more blind reactions. Having a clear and decisive plan to face your fears is like slowly chipping away at the boulder that sits on your chest. You'll feel lighter and more positive in no time. It's how we grow and develop.

Having a clear and decisive plan to face your fears is like slowly chipping away at the boulder that sits on your chest.

Remember that having swagger is the ability to keep your true self intact as it tries to surface through all the crap that will try and keep it hidden. Remove the illusion of massive labors in your way and the task will feel so much less Herculean. If the end goal is to be able to say, "I've got this," then you gotta get this. And you can!

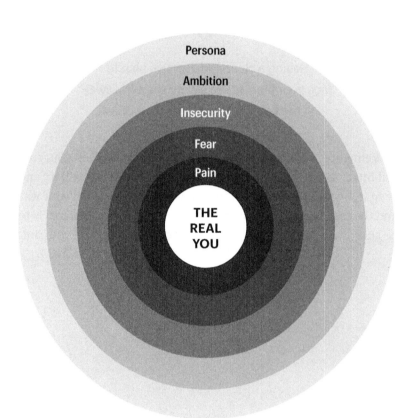

9

PAIN

THE FINAL AND greatest reinforcer of all swagger blockers is *Pain*.

Pain is memory. And it's a mean, unrelenting mutha. Every time we poke our swagger selves out and get a psychological smack in the face, pain is validated, and in turn validates all of the other blockers. Ergo, if no risk is ever taken, pain can't be felt. It's the perfect system for keeping you trapped. But if you want the real you to see sunlight, you have no choice but to chip away at this blocker and start seeing it for the subversive enemy that it is.

There's a reason pain is the blocker that is closest to the real us. Think of it as the final defense, the castle walls that both protect us and separate us from the world. It's also the deepest and thickest, composed largely of seemingly impenetrable scar tissue resulting from memory. You know that giant wall you see in basic training, the one that you have to take a running start at in the hopes that your speed and muscle will get you up and over? That's your visual for transcending pain. Even if we have that chunky rope dangling down—the one we can use to try and pull ourselves up—it won't always help. Getting our swagger past this massive blocker is the greatest challenge. Because it hurts, dammit!

We are all formed by pain. Whereas fear and insecurity can be minimized over time, our pain will always be with us. Not only can pain muffle our truth, but it can also snuff it out given free rein. It doesn't matter whether it's a result of being bullied at school, feeling rejected or unloved, or experiencing loss or trauma—it's all equal and equally valid according to our psyches. A brilliant therapist once told me, "We can never go back in time and remove or fix our pain. But we can learn how to see and respond to it differently when it's triggered." Swagger won't cure your pain, but it can be proof that you've been able to reframe it and, yes, even use it to face the world in all your vulnerable and authentic glory.

PAIN IN ACTION

Understanding how your pain manifests is your first step. Imagine it as a sore spot that never quite heals over. When it's poked or prodded, we react in visceral ways. We can't help it. It's an automatic reflex. My experience as a boxer taught me this in a physical way. While you're supposed to keep your gloves up around your face, if you get a punch to the body, the instinct is to drop your hands to cover the spot. The problem is that the punch has already landed and now you're exposing an even more vulnerable spot. It's a recipe for a knockout blow. Instead, you have to take it and use it as a reminder that while you're vulnerable, you're still standing to fight on.

With regard to swagger, I've seen pain play out in three very distinct ways: defend, distract, or withdraw. When it comes to defending, the boxing analogy also applies. If someone hits you where it hurts, it can really piss you off. The response can have you coming back swinging wildly. Defense and attack go hand in hand. Think about all the times you've been in conflict with someone, regardless of whether it's at work or home. They say something that really stings, and your reaction is to come back with something equally nasty: "Oh, *yeah*? Well, take *that*!" Up go the stakes along with the hurt factor. It all spirals downward from there. Plus, once those words are out of your mouth, they can't be taken back. Apologized for, yes, but eradicated, no. The damage is done. Or, your instinct might be to defend by disputing. Remember when you were a kid and someone accused you of having cooties? "No, I don't! You have *super*-cooties with boogers on top!" was the best clapback ever. I bet that's happened to you in meetings. If someone accused you of being unprepared, you may have shot back with a, "Well, if you had shared the right information with me up front, I might be in a better position to discuss this." That's the business version of the cooties comeback, and it's equally ineffectual.

Trying to distract from the pain can trigger a stream of excuses about why it's not you, why it's not your fault, or, worse, why it's someone else's. This is what I call the "victim response." It ain't pretty. But in our minds, we're just trying to point the activator of our pain at another target so it's not trained on us. While the defend response can make you come across as aggressive or explosive, distracting can paint you in a subtler, uglier light. The people around you start getting paranoid about whether you're going to blame them next and steer clear of working or playing with you. This can really mess with your intention. All you're trying to do is protect your sore spots, but you'll still get labeled as lacking in accountability or, worse, integrity. Yuck.

Lastly, there's the withdraw response. When someone's words or deeds hurt you, you turtle. Head is pulled in, body curls up, and only a shell remains. You sit there taking it, tears prickling or rage seething, but nothing comes out. Or, if the opportunity presents, you bolt, getting as far away from the action as physically possible. Amazing how fast the turtle can run when threatened! But after it's all said and done, you beat yourself up for not saying or doing anything: "What's wrong with me? Why didn't I tell that asshole where to get off? I'm so weak!" (This is usually followed by formulating the perfect response that you will never actually deliver.) Sometimes, it slides into self-distraction, where you tell yourself the story of why the attack was so unfair and unwarranted and should have been directed at someone else. While this may be 100% true, it doesn't help if you won't do anything about it. Turtles can't fight back.

SHUTTING DOWN THE PAIN DRAIN

So what's a person to do? Pain runs so deep, wide, and high that it's really tough to just "get over it." Sheer force of will ain't gonna do it. Instead, some real self-examination, new self-talk, and a plan are all required if we're going to hold on to our swagger.

Ling came to one of my leadership programs as an accomplished tech professional. Chinese-born, she'd migrated to Canada in her mid-thirties and had truly carved out a new life for herself. The proof was all there. I asked her what she wanted to get out of her training experience.

In a whisper she replied, "I want to speak louder." To be honest, I had to lean in to hear her answer.

"Well, that's an easy fix," I thought. I had countless techniques in my toolkit to help with that. But I was wrong.

Pain is not truth.
It's haunted shadows and memories.

What I came to understand was that Ling was the only daughter in a family of four brothers. In Chinese culture (especially during the time she had grown up), women were perceived as second-class, almost disposable entities. As such, she was completely overlooked. Her wants, opinions, and aspirations were ignored. She was told to "stay quiet" for her entire childhood. So she did, becoming progressively invisible—even to herself.

The fact that Ling had been educated was a small miracle. Even when she broke free from her family and made her way to Canada, that silence stayed with her. It was rooted in profoundly painful memory and conditioning. Now, when she was free to speak up for herself, it was too late. She had literally lost her voice.

To make matters worse, every time someone asked her to speak up during a meeting, that memory was triggered and she would recede into her pain.

Ling didn't just need coaching on how to speak from her diaphragm, even though that helped. What she needed was to believe that her voice, words, and ideas had merit. So that's where we worked. I made her the leader of her work team in the program and asked her colleagues to give her the time and space to be heard. I challenged her with taking on the more outrageous parts of their group presentation and sat at the back of the room every time they rehearsed calling out, "C'mon, Ling, let us *hear* you." And we all cheered and clapped when we could.

Slowly but surely, she was able to turn her volume up, and with it came the funny, quirky personality she'd been hiding for so long. Ling didn't just find her voice. She found her importance. Without learning what was triggering her pain, she may have stayed hidden forever. But now, understanding that hearing "speak up" wasn't a criticism of her worth, she was able to lean in and be heard in her own unique, quiet way.

TAKING THE STING OUT OF PAIN

If you can learn to see pain coming, you can step out of its way. Start by trying to figure out your triggers. The secret is to realize that pain comes from the *inside*, not the outside. Thus, no one can actually cause you pain, but you can allow yourself to feel it. Don't get me wrong: there's a lot of hurtful shit out there in the world. But how deeply we allow it to go is within our power. And pain is old. It has memory. So often, what will trigger us isn't the scene playing out in front of us—it's a vivid recall of the first time(s) it was etched in our psyches.

Here's a little exercise I take people through called Dear Loser.

Write a letter to yourself from your inner saboteur, that pain-filled negative voice that screams when triggered. Let it speak the ugliness that you feel inside when the world comes for you. Use strong words and don't pull any punches. Just spew the thoughts you feel are so fucking true that can cause you to lash out, blame, or hide.

It might go something like this . . .

Dear Loser,
You are pathetic. You pretend that you're strong, but the truth is, you're totally spineless. You're not actually good at anything. Your dreams are a fucking fantasy because you know you'll never achieve them. You're not good-looking or smart enough, and you don't have the personality to make your mark in this world. It's only a matter of time before your failings bring you down. Stop kidding yourself, dumbass. Accept that you're a punching bag for the world, because you deserve it. Might as well just lie down and die now and save yourself a shit ton of time and effort.

Ouch!

Once it's all out, read it back to yourself. Record it and play it back. Better still, if you're feeling brave, ask someone who loves you to read it back to you. For best effect, tell them to use their best sneering Grinch voice.

Let the words roll over you and really hear them. Cry if you need to. But face them. This is your negative talk track—your pain personified.

Now comes the good part.

Get yourself a new page. It's time to write your reply, to tell the voice why it's so utterly and completely *full of crap*. Get mad. Because we would *never* accept the shit we say to ourselves if someone else said it to us. The trick here is to refute the voice using cold hard *facts*. Opinions can be challenged, but the facts cannot.

> Dear Inner Saboteur,
> Pathetic? Spineless? I don't fucking think so. Let me tell you how much I've had to survive in order to be standing here today. I've been through [insert the challenges you've overcome here] and I'm still alive and better for it. Not good at anything? Then how the hell have I managed to [insert your accomplishments here, no matter how big or small] if I'm such a loser? And why do [insert names of people who know, love, and respect you] all love and appreciate me? These are my people because I'm an incredible friend, colleague, and professional. In fact, some of them have told me [write down all the lovely things you've heard about yourself]. My dreams are *mine* and no one can ever take them from me. I'm no one's freakin' punching bag. I am a swagger-filled badass who's well on the way to [list those amazing dreams], and no one can stop me. So step off, asshole!

This exercise might sound silly, but let me tell you: *it works*. We need to remind ourselves in very tangible ways that pain is not truth. It's haunted shadows and memories. But if negative tapes are constantly playing in your head, you can't simply expect to turn them off. The key is to record over them.

Go back to your response letter. Grab your phone and open up your voice memo app. See that gorgeous red button in the middle? Hit it and start reading aloud. Feel free to expound and argue, add facts and realities. Watch the recording levels go up and down, capturing your truth. Get mad, get real, and get proud. Now save it. Call your file something that will remind you of what you've done— "Why I'm a Badass" or "Take That, Pain," or whatever works for you.

Whether you do this figuratively or literally (and I do recommend recording it for real), you now have a new inner talk track that can replace your old, evil one. So the next time you feel yourself getting triggered, as soon as the "Dear Loser..." begins, you need to immediately stop the tape: "Wait a second. That's not real. But let me tell you what *is*..." and let the new recording flow. This may require you to leave a meeting and go into a bathroom stall and hit the playback button a bunch of times, but that's totally cool. Remember how long it took for those original tapes to cement. It's gonna take time to replace them with this new, positive version. But it will happen, I promise you. This process will actually retrain your brain. Over time, you'll laugh at the inner saboteur and mock it for being the ineffectual little shit it is.

PAINLESS STRATEGIES FOR PAIN

Now we can make a plan for better deflecting these gut punches before they land.

Write down a specific situation that you know can trigger your defend, distract, or withdraw response. There's a good chance this is something that allows your pain to climb into the driver's seat. Examples might be:

- Someone claims credit for work that I've done.

- My personal or professional integrity gets questioned in public.

- A formal feedback session happens with my direct boss during which I'm unfairly (or even fairly) criticized.

- The quality of my work is shat upon from on high.

Now think about what your usual "pain" response would be in one word. Nail it down. Would you defend, distract, or withdraw? Be honest. For example:

Situation: Someone claims credit for work that I've done.

Response: Defend.

Situation: My personal or professional integrity gets questioned in public.

Response: Withdraw.

Awesome. Do this with a bunch of scenarios. Feel free to use personal and professional examples.

Now look at the patterns. What's your natural "go-to" response? Do you usually come back swinging? Is your instinct to slink away? Or do you get indignant and highlight the faults of others?

Truth time. These reactions will be how people form their opinions of you. We know that we're the most harshly judged when we're at our worst, and pain has a way of bringing out the beast in us. But hopefully you're discovering that this is not the truth about you—it's simply how you go about protecting your heart, which is *so* worthy of protection. So much of pain is not in what *is*, but how it goes in.

So let's examine what's really going on so we can see these shitty scenarios for what they really are—reactions, not reality. Because we can change *any* reaction if we can anticipate, understand, and prepare for it.

Next step, add how the situation would make you feel and why.

Situation: Someone claims credit for work that I've done.

Response: Defend.

Why: Because I'd feel like something was being taken from me, and I'd want to fight back. It's not fair!! They should get as much shit as they're giving to even the score and should be called out for their bullshit.

Great! This should make you feel better because, yeah, it totally sucks when we feel taken advantage of. Good to get that out of your system. But who's going to come out of this worse, you or them? And who has swagger on their side? And who understands what their truth is? It's sure as *hell* not the asshole who's trying to steal your thunder.

So how do we interrupt the reaction? What could or should we say out loud to address that? And when would be the best time? And why do we feel the need to say what we want to say? Later, in the swagger drivers section, you'll learn that questions like these are the secret to keeping your swagger intact in the face of bullshit. But for now, let's just wing it a little.

Under your "Why," write down what you think your best self would do. Pretend you're Gandhi meets Toni Morrison with a dash of Obi-Wan Kenobi thrown in. What behavior would make you so freakin' proud of yourself, even if you can't imagine having the strength of character to do it quite yet? For example:

Situation: Someone claims credit for work that I've done.

Response: Defend.

Why: Because I'd feel like something was being taken from me, and I'd want to fight back. It's not fair!! They should get as much shit as they're giving to even the score and should be called out for their bullshit.

My Best Self Would: Smile enigmatically. I'd actually feel sorry for the guy, knowing he's going to screw himself if anyone expects him to have deep knowledge of the thing I did. And I'd also know that anyone who really knows anything about the work also knows who's really responsible for it. I'd let it roll in the moment, and later, with no animosity, I'd take him aside and ask what that was all about. I'd tell him that it made me sad, that it sucks when anyone takes credit for someone else's work (as I'm sure it would for him), and ask why he needed to do it. No matter what he says, I'll say I understand. And I'll ask that next time, if he feels that he needs recognition or credit, he just come to me in advance and we can figure out how to make it a win for everyone.

You *go*, Gandhi!

You may be miles away from this happy place right now, but even dreaming of it will show you that you can actually feel good in the face of pain. Because these things that hurt us aren't about anyone else: we can choose to feel however the hell we want. I've discovered that this is the secret of many happy people. The "you do you" attitude allows the punches to simply glance off.

So write it down and aspire to it. When and if the situation or something like it arises, capture any new reaction you've developed so you can track your progress. There may be six interim stages between what you would do today and the Zen response of the Best Self of tomorrow, but who cares. We know swagger is a journey, and this is just another step toward it.

Bottom line? Pain will always be with you. Bad shit will happen to you. But living your life trying to avoid it will be a life filled with missed worthwhile risks, adventures, and opportunities. Knowing you can strategize for it means you can survive it. No pain really does mean no gain. If you don't believe that, your swagger will never be the unstoppable gale force you need it to be.

So there you have it, the blockers that separate your real self from the world. Sure, they may seem daunting, but know that with some work, they're totally surmountable. Visualizing them as a series of negotiable barriers as opposed to a confusing and overwhelming mixed bag of issues can make the swagger process feel much more doable. And remember, the real you is waiting there patiently to be released in all of its glory. We just need to give it a little help.

So let's do that.

PART THREE

DRIVING THE REAL YOU INTO THE WORLD

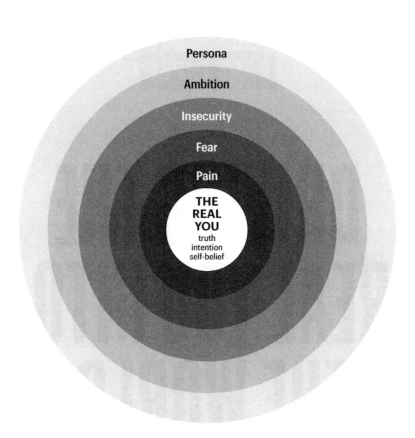

Persona

Ambition

Insecurity

Fear

Pain

THE REAL YOU
truth
intention
self-belief

10

SWAGGER DRIVERS

YOU'LL SEE NOW that sitting at the very core of the real you are three key swagger drivers: *Truth*, *Intention*, and *Self-Belief*.

Truth is what you want and need to express, intention is why you want to express it, and self-belief is knowing that you are the best person to express it now, and that you have the right to, in this situation.

Imagine these drivers as powerful little missiles of authenticity that penetrate your swagger blockers and carry the real you out and then back in to strengthen your core self. They are the bold representatives of who you really are, the advocates for your importance in the world. They are your best and bravest soldiers in the fight for swagger. They also act as your true north by helping you to plan, execute, and manifest your badassery without turning into a cocky shithead. Last but not least, they are a nifty planning tool for facing particularly daunting situations like high-stakes meetings, presentations, sales opportunities, and even relationship discussions.

The biggest challenge you'll face is learning how to keep your truth, intention, and self-belief intact as they navigate through the swagger blockers.

HOW TRUTH, INTENTION, AND SELF-BELIEF OPERATE

Imagine you're in a situation where you're intimidated, but you really, really want to express the truth you know is important both for you and the team, even if it's going to be unpopular—say, a project review or status update. Your good intention is clear in your mind, and you believe not only that this is the right time to say it, but also that you're the best person to say it. Great: that's the perfect setup.

Now imagine that your truth, intention, and self-belief are in a fragile little bubble that has to make its way through a formidable gauntlet of shit in order to reach the surface. Picture it pushing past pain, shadowboxing through fear, zigzagging past insecurity (with its fingers in its ears and singing), dodging the ambition bullet, and breaking through persona to reach the surface. Waaahooo! The crowd goes wild—your swagger has arrived!

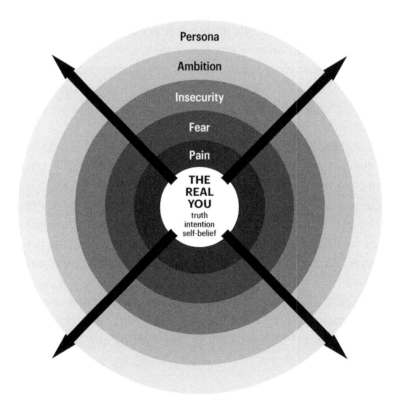

If only it were that easy.

Just the act of negotiating those layers can have a dramatic effect on your bubble. Every barrier has the potential to deflate, puncture, or totally flatten your message. What feels like a warrior cry on the inside can end up a little squeak by the time it reaches the surface, having had the psychological shit kicked out of it at every turn.

But let's say by some miracle you were able to hold on to the core of it and release your invaluable words out into the world. High fives for you! For the benefit of the doubt, let's also assume that your truth was fully appreciated by your audience. All around that meeting table, thumbs were up, faces beamed. Your boss looked at you with the kind of admiration usually saved for someone who's announced the project is coming in before deadline and under budget. You are a freakin' god right now!

Not so fast.

All of that admiration and appreciation now has to work its way back in through those very same blockers in order to fill and strengthen your swagger center (and your resolve).

Let's listen in on what can happen in the process...

Persona: "Crap. I wonder how people are going to see me from now on? I mean, this was so not the *me* they're used to seeing..."

Ambition: "This could totally backfire on me. Now I've put the spotlight on myself, which could make me a target if things go wrong..."

Insecurity: "They all *look* like they liked what I was saying, but I bet half of them are thinking I'm a troublemaker and are going to talk shit about me as soon as they walk out of the meeting..."

Fear: "What have I done? Why the hell did I say anything in the first place? This was a really, really bad idea. I just screwed myself..."

Pain: "This is just like what I did to myself last year when I said something to my boss, then couldn't sleep for a week, and it was brought up in my quarterly review. I'm an idiot. Why do I do this to myself? I am never going to be successful. I might as well stop trying."

Now that sweet little bubble filled with truth, intention, and self-belief, which should have been inflated and impenetrable enough to carry kudos and confidence back inside to grow your swagger core, has become a flat, quivering, ineffectual dishrag that only dampens future resolve.

This scenario can be even more dire if your audience gives you a straight-up beatdown out of the gate.

Just the thought of this can make attaining swagger feel nearly impossible. But it doesn't have to be. Like anything in this world, releasing your swagger requires planning and practice. It's not just a single decision you make. It's trial and error and having the courage to learn from it and continue to stay the course.

Understanding, reconciling, and learning how to communicate with truth, intention, and self-belief can be the key to making your swagger bulletproof, because once it starts to flow, it serves to swell your core self to the max, making it so much more powerful in the fight against swagger blockers. So let's work through each of these drivers one by one.

11

TRUTH

TO BE HEARD in this world, we have at our disposal one invaluable weapon: words. If we speak our truth, we know we are being seen and acknowledged for who we truly are. Truth is the number one driver of our swagger because it has the power to carry our authenticity out into the fresh air for all the world to wonder at. Without truth, we will never know if what's in our hearts and minds is valid.

Not speaking our truth comes at a cost—not just a psychological and emotional one, either. I mean a real dollars-and-cents, bottom-line cost. Just consider every time you chose not to share a potentially game-changing idea because you felt insecure. Or those occasions when piping up could have alerted a decision-maker as to why a project was going off the rails. How about all of the times you held back from expressing to your boss that their words or deeds were killing your productivity and engagement? That shit costs big-time! And it's tantamount to self-censorship, which is a very slippery slope.

Ironically, in so many areas of our lives, bullshit seems easier to swallow than candor. And truth often gets a bad rap, usually by those people who don't have the courage to speak it.

So, who gets to decide whether your words, thoughts, feelings, ideas, or values are important enough to be heard? Granted, truth ain't always gonna be popular. Just ask Galileo. But as soon as you start filtering your truth through the lens of approval, you're actively basing everything you choose to say on things that have been approved of in the past. By definition that means you're never going to change, challenge, or create anything new. Is that the legacy you want to leave? "Oh, that Susie, she sure was approved of a lot. Never rocked the boat, that one. What a good egg." Fuck that six different ways.

Truth is the number one driver of our swagger because it has the power to carry our authenticity out into the fresh air.

Sure, there are inherent challenges to speaking one's truth, but that's why we're here together, to navigate the mountains without falling off a cliff. It's all about the climb, baby.

Let's get the big existential crap out of the way. Truth can be subjective. What is *perceived* to be true can be very different depending on who's doing the listening. Have you ever had a big relationship fight where you believed absolutely that you were pointing out facts, and your partner disputed every single one and threw what you thought was bullshit back at you? Yup—that's the fuzzy nature of "truth." But in this life, it's really all we have if we want to feel that we're expressing ourselves with authenticity. People may not like your truth, but that doesn't mean you shouldn't express it! The trick is to be able to understand where it's coming from and find the best words, and timing, to get the point across. This is why truth isn't a standalone here. It's got to piggyback on intention and self-belief in order to keep it in some kind of check.

Speaking your truth isn't license to run around spewing your opinions or judgments on others, either. It's more an antidote to feeling unheard, misunderstood, or suppressed in some way. If swagger is the authentic manifestation of who you really are, then speaking your truth *must* be in your toolkit if you want to be successful.

THE POWER OF SPEAKING YOUR TRUTH

There are countless reasons why speaking our truth is daunting. Most humans are reasonably sensitive to the feelings of others and worry that real talk could hurt someone else. But being able to express our true feelings or opinions is critical to healthy humanity and our sense of self-worth.

In the business world, we tend to be afraid that truth might bite us in the ass. Is there anything scarier than speaking up about an issue that everyone else seems to be ignoring? Or refuting a review that you feel is unfair? How about calling a superior out for how their behavior is making you feel? That's the stuff of nightmares for most of us.

Fear of speaking our truth is often ingrained in us at a young age and reinforced as we develop. When we're little, it's called "talking back" and the consequences can be anything from dismissive to punitive. At school, it's called being a "loudmouth" or "troublemaker" and usually results in a call to our parents or a visit to the principal's office. Doesn't much matter what our issue is. In relationships, speaking our truth can trigger conflict, withholding of love, or even the severing of ties.

By the time we reach the professional world, we've been pretty much conditioned to hold our tongues and just get on with the status quo. The stakes become high, and we rarely see truth talk modeled to any good end. That's why there's so much water cooler sniping and venting in most workplaces. The truth that needs to be spoken has to come out somewhere, but because it can't find a place to be productive, it seeps out as toxic sludge that benefits no one. A workplace culture of gossip and backstabbing is a result of people's inability to "speak truth to power" and be adequately heard and respected in that environment.

Speaking truth to power has always been a human challenge. The ancient Greeks referred to it as "parrhesia," meaning "to speak candidly or to ask forgiveness for so speaking." Parrhesiastes means "one who speaks truth to power."[7] In the 1950s, the Quakers used the phrase as part of their manifesto to find alternatives to violent actions. Since then, it's become a political rallying cry for everyone from Martin Luther King Jr. to Anita Hill and the #MeToo movement. Why? Because speaking truth when you feel like you're in a position of lesser power and believe there could be serious consequences can be utterly terrifying, regardless of whether the stakes are personal or global.

So, if you're someone who struggles with truth, it doesn't make you "weak" or a "chicken"; it makes you perfectly human. The instincts for survival and self-preservation should never be ignored, but that doesn't mean that they should control you.

When you filter your truth through the lens of approval, you're basing everything you say on things that have been approved of in the past.

I cannot tell you how many times I've uncovered high-level issues during training in my years of working with senior leadership. Every single time I've communicated the problem to senior leadership, they've said something like, "I wish someone had told me" or have been genuinely surprised to hear that people were afraid to speak up. This proves there's a real disconnect going on.

Remember how our reptilian brain reacts to situations for which it has no context or can't predict the outcome of? If we're unpracticed at speaking our truth, the visceral and very physical response we'll have to even the thought of fessing up can keep our best material locked in a psychological box. Heart pounding, hands shaking, sweat pooling. But if we don't find healthy ways to express our truth, we can end up feeling limited, frustrated, and even unloved.

While there may appear to be lots of good reasons to keep your head down at work, there are even more reasons why piping up could provide a major boost to your personal brand and even your position. For anyone in a leadership position, the ability to speak their truth appropriately is one of those skills that can make followers fall deeply in love with them. Being as honest and open as possible makes a person "transparent," which equates with trustworthy. Remember that a leader is *anyone* who has people under their management. Leaders exist at all levels, and all but the most senior still have bosses they have to work under. (And even they likely have a board of directors or shareholders to account to, unless they're business owners.) The fallacy that a title can free you from the fear of speaking truth or speaking truth to power is bullshit. This is a *human* condition, not a positional one.

Finding constructive and well-intentioned ways of expressing things that you believe need to be said can single you out as courageous, forthright, a leader, a voice for the team, and an advocate for progress and success.

Can speaking your truth backfire sometimes? Abso-fucking-lutely. But it's still a better way to live than being locked up and silent. It can also be an indicator of whether you're in the right or wrong place, job, team, or relationship and should always be accompanied by some real reflection. If people can't handle all of your jelly, it may be on them, not you.

In my experience, the pitfalls of speaking your truth can often be less about the *what* and more about the *how* and *when*.

THE WHAT: PRACTICING TRUTH FOR THE BIG SHOW

Besides taking a big breath and going for it, there are tons of ways you can be better at being bullshit-free. It starts with practice. It might sound weird, but many of us are just so used to choosing every single word, holding back, or couching our thoughts and ideas that we wouldn't even know how to form the words. Just like every other change you learn to make, speaking your truth will take preparation. The smart move is to test the waters with no one listening, to develop competence and comfort, and figure out how you actually, honestly *feel* about stuff. Do you even know what your truth sounds like?

Try this exercise to get a feel for it.

1 Create a list of questions that dig into deep truths. The more delicate the questions, the harder they'll be to answer. Some sample questions are:

- What's one thing I would say to my partner to improve our relationship?

- How could I tell my boss that I feel bullied?

- How could I tell my co-worker that their gossiping is affecting my workday?

- What could I say to my team leader to express my fear about how our project is progressing?

- What could I say to my parent to express my frustration about a sibling situation?

- How could I express my gratitude to my mentor without getting too squishy?

- What would I say to my boss if they asked if I felt I was doing a good job?

Let the questions range from the low to high stakes, from personal to professional. You can even write scenarios that have happened in the past that you wish you'd handled differently. Nothing is off-limits. This is for you and you alone.

2 Jot each question down on a strip of paper and throw the strips into a bowl. Once a day, pick one question and set a timer for one minute. (If you initially find this too long, start with thirty seconds and move up from there.)

3 Stand in front of a mirror. Then answer one question, speaking honestly for the full minute—no overthinking, no people-pleasing, no hesitating. Just barf up some truth. Watch yourself in the mirror. Maybe even record it on your phone so you can see or hear it later. Listen to what you're saying when no one is around. Watch your face and notice what your emotional "tells" are. See if your words align with your body language.

All of this is very different from having thoughts swirling around in your head. Having to articulate them is a far more powerful process.

4 After the minute, ask yourself how honest you think you really were. Is there anything you wanted to say that you didn't? Why not? Was a minute too long or too short? Did you imagine who was standing in front of you and listening? Did your heart pound? Did you feel scared or liberated? Was it hard or easy? Was your intention clear? Were you judgmental or compassionate? All of this will help you understand where your truth might be getting stuck and why, and help you build the chops to be tactfully honest to the best of your ability.

5 Keep adding questions to the list and work though them the same way. Don't be afraid to direct some of them at specific people whom you find intimidating or who have the ability to trigger your swagger layers.

Caution: I've done this exercise many times in preparation for difficult discussions. I've noticed that half of the time I end up in tears. Speaking your truth is scary and cathartic in equal measure, and crying is a healthy release. So make sure you do this with enough time to recover. The best news is that by getting the tears out in advance, you're less likely to need them later. This applies equally to anger. Get mad at the mirror, rant and rave in rehearsal, and then come back to the words you want to choose for the big show.

THE HOW: THE DELICATE ART OF TRUTH TALKING

My best piece of advice is to never make speaking your truth solely about you. If what you're trying to communicate isn't of benefit or relevance to your audience, you end up sounding like the teacher from the Charlie Brown cartoon ("Wa wa wah wah wah..."). Despite our best efforts, we mere mortals tend to give a shit most about one thing: *ourselves*. Never assume that your truth matters to anyone else. It's both logical and smart to align what you want and need to express with something that's going to help your listener.

Never make speaking your truth solely about you.

And if you're going to highlight an issue or flaw, you'd better come ready with some kind of a solution. Otherwise, your message may be dismissed as "venting" or "bitching." I always counsel that if you're going to tell someone their baby is ugly, you'd better have some killer beauty secrets ready to share, and fast! Don't forget that if your reptilian brain can be triggered by the fear of speaking your truth, your listener's brain can be equally triggered by hearing it. Make sure that how you're positioning your message doesn't come across as threatening to anyone's well-being.

Some believe that starting with some smoke-blowing statement is enough to set the stage. This can be not only useless but also patronizing if you're only going to follow up with, "but..." It's like the big windup of the bat before you swing it at someone's psyche. So, saying, "I really think you're an awesome manager and I like working for you, but I don't like it when you..." ain't gonna cut it. Instead, try reframing it through the lens of what you want the result to be. If you're about to criticize, expect defense. But if your aim is to provide an opportunity for your boss to get the best out of you, then state it as such. "You're an amazing boss, and I know you're all about getting the best out of your people. That's why I love working with you. I wanted to share a few insights into how to get even more out of me . . ." This connects to knowing your intention when speaking your truth, which we'll dive into in the next section.

Try to take the "you" out of your truth. Separating the person from the issue can make expressing it so much less emotionally loaded. Let's say it's your partner's job to take out the garbage and they constantly forget. Every time you end up lugging that dripping bag to the curb, you're building up resentment, which is going to lead to simmering irritation and petty sniping. Which is wiser to say to them: "When you don't take out the garbage, you make me like your freakin' house slave, and it's pissing me off," or "When the garbage doesn't get taken out, it makes me feel like we're not respecting the division of labor"?

In a work context, it would be the difference between saying to a peer, "When you talk over me in a meeting, you make me feel like I'm less important than you. So, stop it!" and, "When I get talked over in a meeting it makes me feel frustrated and insecure. I wanted to let you know because I know that's not your intention. Could we work on that?" Having this kind of measured objectivity can be hard when you're already pissed, afraid, frustrated, or at the end of your rope. Which leads to the next piece of advice.

Don't wait to speak your truth. The longer you do, the harder it will get. (Caveat: be mindful of context—see the next section.) Once you get more comfortable with it, it should be easier to be spontaneously straight-up. Before you know it, realness will be your default mode. But while the training wheels are still on, try to notice when you're actively *not* speaking up in the moment and immediately start formulating a plan for how and when to do it. Repressing your truth can be like sitting in the corner stuffing cookies down your throat. It may feel good at first, but you get fuller, angrier, and more sluggish in the end. By the time you decide you can't take

ᵣe, your truth may literally spew out of you as bitter bile,
one wants to get all over them. Worse still, you may be so
....ᵤₘ holding it in that you never say it at all.

Do a quick analysis of the situation that you believe requires
or deserves your truth. Now swap chairs and imagine it from the
perspective of the person or people you're hoping will hear it. How
might they feel? How would *you* feel in their position? A little empathy can help you check yourself. While something may be your truth,
it may not actually need to be shared for any other reason than to
make *yourself* feel better. If that's the case—shut it. Go for drinks
with a friend and vent that shit.

Lastly, if you're truly terrified of having a straight-up conversation with someone or making a challenge of some kind, try asking
for permission. I don't mean the obsequious, powerless kind of
permission asking ("Please sir, can I have some more?"). I mean
the direct but unthreatening kind, like, "Hey, I'd really like to talk
about something I feel is getting in the way of my best work on
the team. Would you be open to that?" (See how I snuck that benefit
in there?)

You've got to be equally prepared to receive a hard no, or even a
brush-off. This too can be a wake-up call about your intended audience's level of interest or confidence. That's good info, too, because
you can lead a horse to truth serum, but you can't make 'em drink.
If your truth isn't valuable to the people who matter in your world,
you may want to consider changing worlds, because you sure as hell
can't change people.

THE WHEN: IT'S ALL IN THE TRUTH TIMING

Releasing your swagger isn't about speaking your truth whenever
the hell you want to and expecting people to eat it up. A message shouted in a group can be taken completely differently from
one spoken face-to-face or whispered in an ear. Part of being an
undeniable and irrefutable badass is knowing when (and sometimes
even where) to get things out into the open.

We all know that being criticized, even constructively, in public can be devastating, whereas the same words can go down gently when in private. It's important to assess your situation and surroundings and make quick decisions about whether this is the time or the place to get hoped-for results.

Politics, ego, culture, and relationships can all play a part in your determinations, whether in a work or play situation. The criteria are pretty simple.

Before speaking, ask yourself whether your truth may reflect negatively on the perception of others at that moment. If so, shut your mouth and wait until you have the appropriate person alone in order to achieve your well-intentioned goal—even if the relevant discussion is happening right in front of you. If you don't, trust me when I say that things will likely not turn out well.

Sital, a project manager at a tech firm, told me how she's responsible for identifying issues that might derail her project. It's a key part of her job. When the team met with their business sponsor to update him, she chose that moment to point out some pretty serious issues with the potential to blow things up. Well, things blew up all right, but not in the way she'd hoped. The business sponsor turned on the whole team, accusing them of trying to kill their progress and make the entire project look like it was failing. Forget the fact that she had highlighted something critical that required fixing. Forget that she was looking out for the greater good and the organization as a whole. Forget that it was true. And totally forget the fact that *it's her freakin' job*. None of that mattered. All the business sponsor cared about was that it made him look bad—worse, he looked bad in front of the entire team. Despite speaking her truth, Sital left the meeting with her tail between her legs, shaken up, and in this guy's sights for all the wrong reasons. And the project was no better off than before.

"Well, that guy's just a dick," you might say, and you might be right. But that's not the point. Sital chose the worst moment to reveal her info despite the fact that it was exactly what the meeting was for. Why? Because the words she said and when she said them were totally threatening to this guy's status and well-being. To hell with her intentions. They just didn't matter.

What could she have done differently? For starters, she could have gone to her direct boss and asked for advice and endorsement. She might have learned something helpful about office politics. Her boss would have appreciated her discretion. At the very least, she would have been covering her own ass. She could have connected with the business sponsor in advance (face-to-face or through an email) and shared the info privately, making sure to point out that she didn't think the meeting was the right place to air it. Even if the sponsor didn't like the news, he sure would have appreciated not being publicly blindsided with it. The extra-savvy move would have been to follow up with an email reiterating their conversation so there could be no question as to whether she was being diligent in her role.

Just because things need to be said, doesn't necessarily mean they have to be said *immediately*. When it comes to emotionally charged truths, this is particularly important. If you're all in your feelings about an event, conversation, or emotional injury of some kind, the worst time to speak your truth is when you're still stinging from it. You'd have to be a robot to make that shit come out gracefully. Take a minute, an hour, a day—whatever amount of time you need to step back and think about the best way to handle it. Then find private time with the offender and follow the rules of engagement mentioned earlier. This shouldn't be used as an avoidance tactic; rather, it's a smart strategy for making sure your truth comes out right and can be better accepted by the listener.

The mark of superpowered swagger is being able to hold on to your center in wobbly moments and not panic or react badly. There's no bad truth, but there is poor timing. Make sure you can separate the two for the benefit of everyone.

So remember, speaking truth isn't simply about honesty. There's a series of checks and balances to ensure that your message will fall on the right ears, in the right place, and at the right time. Take heed of them, practice, plan, and execute wisely. Otherwise your truth may fall flat—and that will be on you more than on the audience.

12

INTENTION

INTENTION IS EVERYTHING. It is the "why" of your swagger and can mean the key difference between cocky and confident, separating soulful from soul crushing, and keeping integrity firmly in place. Intention also serves as a kind of unimpeachable armor for your truth that helps carry your swagger past the blockers and through to your audience intact. Without it, swagger can veer into asshole territory and justify anything you say or do in the name of "authentic expression." (And if you're authentically being an asshole, then you deserve everything you get.)

In worst-case scenarios, and if it's genuine, intention can act as a "get out of jail free" card. We're human. We screw up—say, do, think, and act the wrong way. But if it's for the right reasons, we hope to be forgiven.

Sharing your intention up front can do wonders to prepare your listener for what's coming, especially if the conversation is going to be touchy or delicate. For example, "I know you're having a really hard time these days and it's affecting you badly. My intention here is to help in any way I can because I know you're getting some harsh judgment about it." That's a juicy, well-intentioned conversation starter. Be careful, though: don't state intention with the "but ..." we talked about in the truth chapter. Saying, "I just want to help you and it's all about love, but you're really behaving like an idiot" is an unsanctioned move in the game of intention. Of course, the listener will feel both blindsided and attacked, which won't end well for either party.

**If genuine, intention can act as
a "get out of jail free" card.**

Intention also serves to provide focus for words and actions. In my years of presenting to rooms filled with clients and decision-makers, I've always found it useful to state my intention. It's like slipping a lens of context over their eyes to make sure they see what you're trying to show them. It's a little sneaky, because once you tell people to see something, they have a hard time unseeing it.

For example, if I were taking them through a creative advertising concept at the early stages, I would explain my intention of making consumers feel a certain way, or what I was hoping to accomplish for the brand or business. By being super-clear about my "why," it helped them share my vision, even if it was a little fuzzy going in. That way, although they might not have loved the actual idea, they'd always buy into what I was trying to do. That kept the conversation wide open and positive on both sides, which resulted in better outcomes for everyone.

In meetings or business presentations, knowing your intention can help you properly prepare your materials and set up your truth and ideas for success. If you're clear on the purpose of what you're doing, it tells you what should stay in or out of your agenda or deck. Do this by assessing what their needs, fears, or desires might be and then genuinely give them what would satisfy or alleviate their issues. Whether you say it out loud to them (and I often recommend that you do), ask yourself what your intention is for them and your outcome. For example, "My intention here is to make them feel so comfortable with the budget I'm proposing that they'll be happy saying yes." Cool. Then do that. Don't get off track and meander into any other territory. Show them costs, benefits, and any supporting proof they need. Don't waste their brain and heart space with updates and extraneous content. If you do this well, you can use that to set up their expectations: "My intention today is to make you feel really comfortable with the numbers." It also helps stop them from trying to take you down rabbit holes of their own agendas. There's always one shit disturber who's gonna pipe up with, "Yeah, but what about the project we did last year…" Take that pain in the ass right back to your intention. "No problem. If we want to dig into that, I can get the details to you. Today, my intention is just to run the cost and benefits of this project."

Sometimes we're put in situations where the "ask" is fuzzy. We know we have a responsibility to communicate something to our boss, peers, or a wider audience, but we're not crystal clear on what they really want, need, or expect from us. So, own it. Use the fuzziness to your advantage. Intention can be your opportunity to ask for permission and affirmation from your listeners: "My intention here is to help you understand how we made the decisions around the user experience. Is that going to be helpful for you today?" If heads nod, you're good. If they don't, stop and ask for clarity. If you just plow through, your listeners are not just going to tune out, they'll also probably be pissed that you're wasting their time. Half of the time, people have no freakin' idea why they've been invited to a meeting in the first place. Intention can be that great level set.

But my absolute favorite thing about intention, and why I believe it's a key swagger driver, is that it really will help you to keep your own shit correct. Sometimes we kid ourselves about what we want. You tell yourself that you're trying to be of service to others, but you're really trying to feed your own ego or further your agenda. People can smell that from miles off. I've been guilty of both faking my intention and not realizing what it actually was until it was almost too late. I've learned that before I put my stake in the ground with *any* interaction, I need a quick check-in with my intention. It's likely why I've been given permission to use the kind of wild and crazy tactics in my workshops that I do. Because my clients understand that my pure intention is to get the best out of humans, I'm forgiven a lot of shtick. And I know for sure that it's helped me have healthy personal relationships, big-time.

Having clarity on your intention can make a world of difference when you're facing big challenges, too. If you're running a marathon, is your intention to beat your own time or everyone else's? If you're trying to lose weight, is your intention to be slimmer or healthy? If you're changing jobs, is your intention to run away from a problem or take on a new challenge? Getting your intention right ensures your swagger can help you ride out the bumps in real time. Otherwise, you start doubting yourself at mile eighteen, when other runners are passing you; get pissed at the scale when your body type doesn't change; or go into interviews with a chip on your shoulder.

**Knowing your intention will
help you to keep your own shit correct.**

My greatest learning experience about intention came on the heels of one of these massive challenges.

In 2014, I started boxing. Suffice it to say that I think it's the most incredible sport on the planet. There is nothing more liberating than knowing that you can take a solid punch in the face, smile through it, and keep planning how you're going to land your own shots. Surprisingly, every lesson I learned in the gym had an application to my professional life, and I discovered new insights and wisdom every day. And boxing people rock. You gotta love someone who lets you hit them in pursuit of your own excellence.

For me, in the beginning, it was just a badass form of fitness and I loved the funky, sweaty camaraderie of the environment. I'd never actually considered climbing into the ring for real.

But all that was about to change.

My boxing gym was the founder of a cancer charity fundraiser called Fight to End Cancer. The premise is that ten white-collar professionals are intensively trained as Olympic-style boxers for six months and then have their debut fights at a black-tie fundraising gala—all in the name of raising money for urgent cancer research and medical support. I'd watched my gym buddies take part in the event, and it scared and elated me.

So, in 2015, at fifty years old, I tried out. Miraculously, I was invited to be part of the fight team, and I endured the most grueling and humbling regime of my life.

For the next six months, I faced the specter of swagger every single day. I was on the receiving end of some serious beatdowns, when only the sweat pouring off my face could mask a flood of tears. The second I thought I actually had some "game," someone would catch me in a rookie move and put me in my place—on my ass. Other days, I felt like freakin' Rocky and would strut around the ring with my fists raised, theme song playing in my head. I doubted my stamina, my technique, my resolve, and even my body. Through it all, I was aware that I had never felt so vulnerable and revealed. My shit was truly laid bare on a daily basis, and my trainer, Virgil, would hug me, school me, and scold me through it. I wanted to quit about five times and fortunately recovered six.

You should know that I'm an incredibly competitive person. I wanted to win my fight so badly it made my teeth hurt. My intention was beyond clear. I visualized, pep talked, pumped up, and focused my ass off. Win, *win*, WIN! My fundraising efforts had reached almost $30,000, and I knew I was as ready as I'd ever be.

And then fight night came.

I was standing outside the vast wooden doors of a posh hotel ballroom. I could hear an eager crowd and the thumping of music that sounded only slightly louder than the thump of my heart in my ears. I probably should mention that I was wearing headgear, boxing gloves, and the most unflattering shorts on the planet. I was fifty-one years old and about to fight my first sanctioned amateur boxing match.

Inside were friends, family, and colleagues. There were CEOs and politicians, celebs and community leaders. And I was about to step into the ring with all eyes on me. I was shit-scared—though not because I was afraid of the fight. I was ready for it. But I was afraid to lose. That's the truth of it. My intention to win had completely taken over. Nothing else mattered.

The wooden doors swung open. Flashing lights and the roar of the rowdy crowd sent my already jacked-up adrenal system into overdrive. Virg was in front of me, swinging a towel to lead me through the waiting crowd. LL Cool J's "Mama Said Knock You Out" blasted from the speakers. I absently heard cheers and felt pats of supports as I went by. Up the stairs I went, and Virg held the ropes to ease my entry into the ring. My heart hammered. I heard my opponent making her way to the ring with equal ceremony.

And then it all got quiet in my head for a second. I took in the room, the excitement, the faces. "Holy shit," I thought. "This is it. I'm really doing this." And that's when I realized: I wasn't just "doing this"; I had already done it. To get to that moment had required me to be fearless, real, and to let go of any ego bullshit I was carrying around. I had raised nearly $30,000 for a cause I believed in. My swagger was complete because it actually didn't matter whether I won or lost! The only difference was that after the bout, I'd go from boxer to fighter.

For a second, I was unsettled. Wait—did I not want to win anymore? What was this voodoo? In a flash, my intention had changed from the pure white fire of competitiveness to one of celebration. Now I just wanted to be present in the experience. My true intention had been waiting for me to find it. I just hadn't been paying attention.

The referee called us to the center of the ring for rules of engagement. I stared up at my opponent, as she was at least five inches taller than me and had arms the length of a freakin' ballplayer.

Then the bell rang.

Six minutes later, it was over. She'd clearly taken one round, and I'd squeaked through one myself. The third was up for grabs. Back in the center of the ring, the ref held each of our arms, waiting for the judges' results.

And you know what? I didn't care what they were.

I don't think I'd ever felt the kind of elation I felt in that moment. I was a total *badass*. I had done it—cellulite hanging out from my stupid shorts and all. I could hear my mom, my husband, my friends screaming for me. I was so alive and totally, completely, unapologetically me. I had already won.

The ref raised my opponent's arm, and I swung around to grab her in a huge hug. We held on for a bit as the crowd cheered.

In that moment, I was completely and utterly content. In the nick of time, I'd realized that if I'd held on to my bullshit intention of winning, I'd have lost so much more than just the fight. Righting my intention before it was too late let me win the battle for my swagger in the end. And what a sweet victory that was.

BEING UNAPOLOGETIC ABOUT INTENTION

The final word on intention is about what to do when others question or challenge it. Do you stand up or stand down? What's the difference between being unapologetic about your intention and apologizing for the outcome?

When other people feel that we've hurt them, they often start brokering for an apology. They see the apology as an acceptance or agreement that the behavior that injured them was wrong. But here's the rub: sometimes it is, and sometimes it *isn't*. Being expected to apologize means that you're allowing someone else to dictate the intention of your behavior. The "I'm right and you're wrong, thus you should apologize" is a direct play for your power. It's important to analyze it as such before you make a decision as to how to act on it.

Ask yourself, "What would I be apologizing for?" Choosing to be unapologetic requires you to have a clear understanding of what your intention is at all times. This means that you've assessed a situation and have spoken your truth, regardless of how popular or unpopular it may be. While others may not have liked it, it doesn't change your intention. But as soon as you apologize, it means you're questioning your intention. And that shouldn't happen. There's a huge difference between "I'm sorry that I said that" and "It was not my intention to upset or hurt you."

Being expected to apologize means allowing someone else to dictate the intention of your behavior.

Save apologies for an unintended injury to values. People will react in the most emotional ways when they feel their core values have been challenged or hurt. When our intention is good, we're often unaware that we've upset someone and are surprised by the visceral reaction we get. So what to do? Start by explaining your intention so you can learn more about their values. Then, if you discover that you've inadvertently tromped all over them, choose whether to apologize for the result, but not the intention. It's kind of like when we apologize after someone else bumps into us. Even if we weren't the "bumper," it acknowledges a middle ground of shared impact.

Important note here: if your clear intention is ever to hurt, diminish, or control others, then you are fair game for whatever comes your way. To reclaim any ownership of swagger, it will be your job to right that wrong—because all of that *is* hella wrong. Suck it up, say sorry, mean it, and do better next time.

Know your intention, folks. It's the compass for your swagger, and you should always know exactly in which direction it's pointed.

13

SELF-BELIEF

THE FINAL SWAGGER driver is an epically powerful one. The ability to believe in one's self is tough, and it's the driver most likely to falter when facing down swagger blockers.

What also makes self-belief challenging is that it literally must come from the *self* rather than being a reflection of other people's belief in you. The old "you can do it" pep talk that a supporter may offer doesn't apply here. Decisions to speak your truth and be secure in your intention have to come from the inside, and often in the moment. If your self-belief isn't firmly in place, you won't have the vital intrinsic support you'll need to make those decisions. Instead, you'll hesitate, doubt, and usually err on the side of what you see as caution.

Make no mistake. Self-belief is vastly different from confidence. Confidence comes as a result of competence, which implies you've had lots of experience in the exact skill or situation, like executing your work or presenting in front of people. After you've done those things countless times, you'll develop a sense of assuredness that bad things won't result; thus, your fear and insecurity will minimize. And while over time you might need to lightly tap into your swagger to deliver on these skills, you'll also be able to lean on the hundreds or thousands of hours that have proved to your brain that it's all gonna be OK.

Self-belief, on the other hand, is so much more badass because it relies purely on the courage and willingness to step into the unknown over and over again. Whenever you make the decision to speak your truth in new situations, there will be uncertainty. There's no approved process plan, no guidebook. People may dig it, or they may not. We all know speaking one's truth ain't always popular. Self-belief is the unerring faith that you are the right person to express this thing in this moment, for these people and this situation. But how the hell do you really, truly know for sure?

**Self-belief relies on the courage
and willingness to step into the unknown
over and over again.**

My favorite analogy for self-belief comes from an old-school cartoon. Remember how Wile E. Coyote would chase after the Road Runner with absolute commitment and gusto? He'd charge up the winding mountain path, trying to catch a bird that could take corners at breakneck speed. Inevitably, the poor sap would careen over the edge and find himself suspended in midair. He'd hang there for a moment. *And he would fall only when he looked down.* That's the secret to self-belief: Never. Look. Down. Instead, believe with all of your being that if you speak your truth and act with intention, that path through midair will magically reveal itself beneath your feet. Trust me, this works.

I wish I could provide you with some kind of exercise to practice self-belief. There just isn't one. Self-belief is a leap you'll have to take over and over. The good news is that it is the element of the Mighty Swagger Triumvirate that will naturally strengthen and deepen over time as you practice truth and intention. You'll just start feeling your badass self more and more. And once you do, that gorgeous sensation will be such an important driver for freeing your real self and completing the swagger journey.

However, there is a mental process that can help. When we need to tap into our swagger, there are a few quick, rational check-ins we can go through to solidify self-belief.

Truth: What is the message to be communicated, how best can I phrase or frame it, and is the timing right?

Intention: What's my honest intention? What am I hoping to achieve that will not just serve me, but also be beneficial to the collective in some way? (Remember, your truth doesn't have to make life easier for others, but it should provide value in the long run, even if it's just in the form of giving people better insight into you.)

Self-belief: Do I believe that I am the best person to express this, and that I have a right to express it here and now despite what others may think?

First, keep in mind that when it comes to self-belief, no one can argue with it. You either believe yourself or you don't. Also, remember that self-belief is in reference to *your* truth, not *the* truth. That makes it unimpeachable. For example, Oprah has shared countless examples of "What I Know for Sure," and while these might be super-valuable to us mere mortals, it's still a representation of *her* truth based on *her* experience. What *I* know for sure is that Oprah gives zero shits about whether or not anyone else agrees with her. She knows exactly what her intention is in sharing it. That's swagger in action.

Having a quick series of checks and balances is extremely helpful when you're trying to solidify self-belief. Yes, we all face insecurity. Yes, we're all afraid. But that's the whole point. Self-belief is about feeling the fear and doing it anyway because you know deep down that you and your truth are worth the risk! That *knowing* is key. And trust me, you are worth it. That's swagger in action. So, yes, feel what you're feeling, but also apply some rationale to your process. Have a moment of self-talk to separate your thoughts from your emotions so the best parts of your brain can serve you.

A positive and productive example of an internal assessment for self-belief might go something like this:

Q: Am I clear on my truth and intention in the situation?

A: Nope. Hold, please! *Then go on to reassess your truth and intention.*

A: Yup. Good to go. Tick! *Get down with your bad self.*

Q: Is there anyone else here who I believe is better suited to express this truth?

A: Hmm . . . if I know I'll truly be talking out of my ass, then I should trust that inner voice and rethink. *Wise idea.*

A: Even if I'm not an "expert," I believe I can use this opportunity to learn and help others learn, so what the hell! *Go for it.*

Q: Am I relying on the courage or willingness of others to speak the same truth because it needs to be said? Could I be doing a disservice by not doing it myself?

A: I can't let culture or politics get in the way of my truth. So why not me? I'm willing to take one for the team!! *Banzai!!*

Q: Do I think I will be more successful, happier, and more fulfilled for simply having spoken up—regardless of the outcome?

A: By speaking up, not only am I giving myself a gift by expressing my truth once and for all, but also it could improve my relationships with these people in the long run. If I've done my best, spoken with truth and intention, and they take it badly, that's on them, not me. *Go on with your swagger self!*

Q: Am I withholding or hiding my authenticity by not speaking?

A: If this is a true swagger moment, I've got to walk the talk. If I don't, I'll continue to hide my true self and that's not good for anyone. *Word.*

Q: Am I allowing my concern over what people might think of me, or fear of repercussions, to silence or change me?

A: Ohhh, man, am I ever getting stuck in fear and insecurity. I can't live my life based on the subjective opinions of others. Come on, swagger—we have work to do! *Just DO it!*

Q: What are the factual reasons to not believe in myself right now?

A: If there is absolute proof as to why I should not believe in my position as truth-speaker in this moment, then I should stop and regroup before proceeding. The likelihood is that my self-limiting beliefs are my biggest hurdle. If my truth and intention are correct, then the only way I'll evolve is by testing my swagger. *Self-belief activated!*

For the record, it's OK if moments when you rely on self-belief don't go as planned. That's life. Wile E. Coyote always lives to chase another Road Runner. The trick is to not get gun-shy about it. We learn from every situation we're in—good or bad. Believing in yourself is the foundation of accomplished dreams. And know this: if you don't believe in yourself, ain't no one else gonna do it for you.

When I started my first training company, I had no idea what I was doing. Seriously. But my truth was that I knew training had to be powerful and exciting enough to provide a transformational experience for people. My intention was to help them be better and happier in their work the very next day. And self-belief? Well, it sure didn't come from any practical experience or proof other than watching people struggle at the companies I'd worked for and desperately wanting to be of service to them. I had no adult learning background, no education or certification on building workshops, and no proven chops as an entrepreneur. But man, did I believe in myself. Because—why not me? There was no factual evidence to make me assume I would fail. I knew that by taking the risk, I was opening up a world of possibility for not only myself, but also the people I would train. I recognized that there was a real need for authentic, soulful, and meaningful learning experiences in the workplace. I knew that I was a powerful communicator. Beyond that, I was diving into the abyss. It wasn't about confidence, competence, or credibility. It was trusting in a burning passion that made it impossible to choose otherwise. And it was fucking terrifying... until it wasn't. That's self-belief in action. (For the record, it turned out pretty well.)

So, in any moment of flagging self-belief, ask yourself that one perfect question, the one that's gotten me through countless moments of indecision: *Why not me?*

If you come up with reasons, knock them down one by one like we did in the Q&A earlier. Keep at it. Be relentless in your pursuit of self-belief. But never expect it to come to you neatly packaged as towering confidence. It might be scary, but if you trust it, self-belief will be the fuel for your swagger fire.

14

TRUTH, INTENTION, AND SELF-BELIEF IN ACTION

THE RECIPE FOR swagger is having your truth, intention, and self-belief clearly and firmly in place and using them to penetrate, face down, and move through your blockers.

THE
REAL
YOU
truth
intention
self-belief

Once all of the pieces are firmly in place, the real you will swell to epic proportions and move effortlessly out and in through those blockers like a laser. Trust and believe that when this happens, your swagger will flow like a mighty river, and there ain't nothin' that can stop it. But when even one of the elements is out of whack, unclear, or turned way down, things can turn out very differently than planned.

My favorite example of this comes from Laura Gassner Otting— aka LGO to her friends, fans, and followers. LGO is an undeniable badass. She served as a presidential appointee in Bill Clinton's White House, founded her own nonprofit recruiting firm, and went on to become a successful speaker and author of bestselling books, including *Limitless: How to Ignore Everybody, Carve Your Own Path, and Live Your Best Life*. She runs marathons and is a competitive rower, intrepid world traveler, activist, and super-involved parent. And she totally knows how to rock a pair of leather pants.

Anyone would think that swagger would be second nature to her. But even for people like LGO, when truth, intention, and self-belief are out of balance, there will be swagger slippage. Like everything she does, LGO experienced this on a big scale—on national TV.

"The first ever TV interview I did—like in my whole life—was on *The TODAY Show*. It was to promote my book *Limitless*. And when *The TODAY Show* calls, you don't say no. Even when they tell you that the audience is predominantly stay-at-home moms and you think you've written a business book and wonder how you're going to make it relevant to them, you still don't say no. Because it's *The Fucking TODAY Show*. You just decide to do what you can do to shove your business book of a square peg into the round hole of their self-help audience."

From the get-go, LGO was unsure of how to embrace her swagger in this setting.

"Was this going to be an authentic manifestation of who I really am?" she asked. "Hardly. I didn't have all the pieces of swagger in place going in."

But what she did have was an amazing support team from the show, from the producers and hosts, who all did their best to set her up for success. Despite that, LGO still knew that only she could grab the Mighty Swagger Triumvirate of truth, intention, and self-belief—except she couldn't. So she asked for help.

"I didn't know what I was doing, so I listened to the producer, who guided me toward being softer in my messaging. I didn't know what to wear, so I listened to my stylist and was softer in my clothing choices—nothing sleeveless, muted tones, even pantyhose! I didn't know how to move, but luckily the segment was done sitting on couches."

(For the record, I can tell you from knowing LGO personally, all of this is *not her*.)

"We had a lovely chat. You know, the kind when you're meeting your future in-laws for the first time. It was great. They were great. I was as great as I could be. Only I wasn't sure I'd been fully 'me,'" she says. "And I don't think I sold a single book. What's worse, I actually got emails from people who saw me on the show and then signed up for my newsletter that the force of energy and language in it was offensive to them. Seriously, one email said that 'the articulate young woman' that they saw in the morning didn't match the 'foul-mouthed brute who would use H-E-Double-Hockey-Sticks.'"

So what the H-E-Double... fuck it. So what the HELL happened?

While LGO felt her truth, intention, and self-belief were clear in her mind, she had a hard time putting them into action in an environment and with an audience that was foreign to her. Her truth, while unshakable, lost some of its context. Her intention, while nothing but good, may have been out of sync with her target. And her self-belief? Frankly, not so much in this scenario. Not only could she not feel it in the moment, but the world appeared to agree.

Fast-forward two months. By then, she had been a guest on more than 125 podcasts, spoken on countless stages, and received endless feedback from readers who had been moved by her speeches and writing. With every talk, meet-and-greet, and interview, LGO's clarity on her truth, intention, and self-belief regarding *Limitless* had crystallized. And then came the call.

"I got invited on *Good Morning America* by my 'shero' herself, Robin Roberts, who'd read my book and was moved by it. But by this time, I'd learned what my book was really about—helping people get out of their own way and really find and embrace their own power. In fact, it *was* a self-help book! The best way for me to do that was to role model it by showing them my power. I knew I had to get on that stage and live in my swagger—not by tamping myself down and being polite, but by taking risks."

> 66
>
> ## I knew I had to get on that stage and live in my swagger—not by tamping myself down and being polite, but by taking risks.
>
> —LAURA GASSNER OTTING

With her truth, intention, and self-belief back in the saddle, LGO knew exactly what to do to ride that pony to success. Even after the producers told her that what she planned to do might be "dangerous," LGO went full-tilt boogie.

"There was movement, energy, interaction," she said. "Asking audience questions on live TV? Flinging a ballot box away with no cares? Doing an Oprah-style book giveaway? Sure, why the hell not? I even chucked those pantyhose for pants. I was the true manifestation of who I am. I was 100% that bitch: pure, unfettered LGO. While I was honored to be on *The TODAY Show*, I was effective on *Good Morning America*."

By the time LGO went to bed that night, *Limitless* was No. 121 of all of the ten gazillion books on Amazon.

The lesson here? Don't lose hope if your swagger slips. It takes time and practice to be able to quickly and easily clarify your drivers each and every time. You'll get it wrong, adjust, try, and try again. Your truth may require reframing. Your intention may need adjusting. And your self-belief may require a little wake-up call. But who gives a shit? Swagger's a journey with ups and downs, ebbs and flows, rodeos and shit shows. But never, ever give up. Like LGO, when it all clicks into place, you'll *know* you've nailed it.

Her advice? "If you want to discover your swagger, go to the very edge of what you see as your incompetence and just keep going. Every inch you go past that is where you'll start to find your swagger."

WHAT'S YOUR SWAGGER MANTRA?

Here's a quick exercise that can bring your truth, intention, and self-belief into clear focus. While we know that these elements will adapt to each unique situation, it's handy to have a big-picture mantra to center ourselves. You can use it just as you would a meditation.

> Fill in the blanks.
>
> I am a _____ whose intention it is to always _____ , and I believe in myself because _____ .

Here's mine as an example.

> *I am a crazily passionate human whose intention it is to always provoke and inspire people into change, and I believe in myself because I know I was born to do this.*

In the face of doubters, haters, and my own monkey brain, I'll repeat this mantra as a reminder of my purpose. It really helps that I don't have to make it up on the spot, too!

So, take a minute or two, think about it, and fill in those blanks with honesty and clarity. Then keep it somewhere you can easily access it—whether it's on a Post-it on your mirror, a screen saver, or even custom-printed on a freakin' coffee cup. Do you, Boo. Because when the going gets tough, the tough sometimes need reminders. Even us swagger warriors.

PART FOUR

WALKING, TALKING, AND FEELING YOUR SWAGGER

15

LIVING IN YOUR SWAGGER SKIN

WE ARE ALL born with physical quirks, nuances, and differentiators. That's what makes the breadth of humanity so freakin' gorgeous. Yet most of us develop a serious hate-on for the very things that make us memorable and unique. (Thanks, adolescence. You fully suck.) We believe we're too tall, too big, or too small. Our skin is the "wrong" color, our accent is "weird" or hard to understand. Our sexuality or gender identification makes us feel like a lonely castaway floating in a sea of "normal." All the shit we cannot change becomes our burden when it could become our guiding light.

As the great RuPaul says, "If you can't love yourself, how the hell you gonna love someone else?" I'd add to that, "And how the hell you gonna get others to love you?" Isn't that what we all we want—to be loved and accepted for who we are in all of our perfectly idiosyncratic glory?

For the record, this concern for a persona of perfection never goes away. Apparently, when Oprah was nominated for an Academy Award for her brilliant work in *The Color Purple*, she almost didn't attend the ceremony, and when she did, she actually hoped that she wouldn't win because she was worried that she looked "too fat" in her dress. Seriously. Oprah.

I've seen this manifest in CEOs and interns alike. The physical unchangeable stuff of us can be a constant source of angst and self-loathing. We convince ourselves that if we look and sound perfect, we can fool others into believing that we are perfect. Except that we aren't, and we can't, and there's no such thing as perfection. "Normal" is an equivalent fallacy, not to mention boring as hell.

Can you imagine what the other horses said when they first saw a unicorn? "What is that *thing* growing out of its head? Look away, Seabiscuit, look away!" But that's just the thing. What makes a unicorn so irresistible and unforgettable is its differentiator. The lesson here is to embrace the physical yumminess that we can't change and instead turn it into our swagger advantage!

WEARING YOUR UNIQUENESS WITH PRIDE

I worked with a female senior executive at Google who is incredibly tall. Like, mega-tall—she is literally head and shoulders above all the dudes in the room. She has a gorgeously deep voice and a strong Eastern European accent. She is strong and smart and kind. Guess what she wanted my help with? How to appear smaller when she was in front of audiences. This glorious specimen wanted to take up *less* space because she believed her height made her intimidating. Sure, I was happy to show her some tricks about where to place herself during video conferences so she could feel more comfortable. But I spent the bulk of our time together persuading her to reframe how she believed others perceived her. Without that, she would always fall victim to her swagger blockers no matter how perfectly she was framed on camera or where she was in the room.

Eventually, I set up a little impromptu survey among her colleagues. "Tell me three words that immediately come to mind when I say her name," I asked them all. Without hesitation, they said words like "strategic," "brilliant," "leader," "badass," and so on. There wasn't even a vague height-specific synonym or inference among them. When I reported this back to her, she was shocked and surprised. "It's just not how they see you," I told her. "You are so much more than a tall girl to them. It's time to let that go and embrace *all* of your badass self."

After that, we focused on how to use her body to eat up a room—how she could cover a stage in just a few strides and super-connect with an entire room. I had her spread her arms in expansive gestures, and make powerful eye contact without tilting her head down too much. I dubbed her "The Mighty Contessa" and worked with her to seriously own that shit. Watching her step back into her body and discover its potency was a very powerful experience for both of us. Through this, she was so much more confident in expressing her truth, intention, and self-belief, without stumbling over a blocker at every turn.

**Swagger means going beyond mere acceptance
of all your quirks and idiosyncrasies into
embracing and celebrating the shit out of them.**

Another classic example of the "quirk-hating" phenomenon comes from a leadership program I was running for a major bank. It was there that I encountered one of the most delightful humans I've ever had the privilege of working with.

Eglys was Venezuelan-born, bubbly, bright, and badass, and she stood out to me right away. I remember thinking, "Wow, this one has *alll* the stuff." But within the first workshop, I discovered that Eglys was hyper-self-conscious about her relatively thick Spanish accent. Turns out she'd been told by some senior leaders that the "way she spoke was minimizing her executive potential." It's probably worth mentioning that English was in fact her *third* language, as she was fluent in both Spanish and French.

"The problem was," she said, "that I didn't sound the same as they did. Obviously, I couldn't communicate in English the way I do in Spanish. I can be very hard on myself, and being criticized for something I couldn't change—well, I just beat myself up over it. My vocabulary felt limited, which then made me rely on 'business-speak' way too much. But what could I do? I was just there, stuck."

My approach was to quickly get Eglys up on her feet to tell stories in front of the group. I'd give her little bits of feedback on how to use her body and voice to best effect, but mostly I just gave her space to wow the room. And wow she did. See, what she hadn't really begun to understand about herself was just how charismatic she was. And she was *funny*! Sure, she mispronounced a few words. Sure, she stumbled every once in a while. But it all added to her immense charm. She had the group howling with laughter, leaning in, and listening intently. They would have followed her anywhere.

"This is you," I told her. "You are not an accent. You are incredible. Your swagger comes from your whole story, and the fact that you are an accomplished Spanish-speaking Latina woman in an English-speaking world is just a small part and a huge testament to that. You sure as *hell* have everything it takes to be a great leader. Fuck the haters."

I'm a smart, capable, strong Latina woman.
And I'm able to walk the talk of diversity and inclusion
and prove that you can be a leader no matter how you speak.

—EGLYS

From that moment on, she became the Sofía Vergara of the group—a proud Latina powerhouse. She worked that accent to the bone. Instead of apologizing when she mispronounced a word, she was the first to make a joke out of it. And when it came time for final group presentations to an audience of senior executives, she brought the house down.

Not surprisingly, Eglys was promoted to an executive position during the program. "It was all about liberation and acceptance," she said. "And it became fun because I just said, 'Fuck it. I don't sound the same as you, but you can understand me, right? So, I can get my ideas across and inspire you just like anyone else.'"

As she embraced her swagger, dropped the business bullshit persona, and rejected the perception that she was "less than" due to her accent, Eglys started to take more risks.

"The opportunity to speak on panels and onstage had come in the past, but I always said no because I thought I was going to sound foolish," she said. "Now I've stopped saying no. Once you've said yes and seen that you didn't die in the process and that things actually went really well, you're like, 'Oh yeah—I can do this!' Then people start calling you for more stuff. Best of all, this gave me the opportunity to show others that they can do it, too."

"I've had people from different countries come up to me after an event and with their thick accents say, 'Oh my God, this is the first time I've seen a leader who doesn't speak perfect English. It's the same as me! It tells me having an accent is fine.' I helped them see that it wouldn't impede their careers. I'm a smart, capable, strong Latina woman. And I'm able to walk the talk of diversity and inclusion and prove that you can be a leader no matter how you speak."

Remember, there is no one ideal version of swagger. It doesn't discriminate. And for the real you to shine, it has to be the *real* you, not some glossy manufactured version. Otherwise, what's the point? Swagger means going beyond mere acceptance of all your quirks and idiosyncrasies into embracing and celebrating the shit out of them.

As Oscar Wilde said, "Be yourself. Everyone else is already taken."

16

SPEAKING OF SWAGGER

HOW WE EXPRESS ourselves reveals who we are and how we think and feel about the world around us. What else can carry our swagger out into the universe? That's why the language choices we make are so important. And believe me: it is all about choices.

The words we speak (and write) can inadvertently define us as "uptight" or "cool," accessible or inaccessible, confident or insecure. Whether we're aware of it or not, we all have little tells and quirks that ironically speak louder than what our intention might actually be. Our truth, intention, and self-belief can be formed one way in our minds, and then, as they go through the meat grinder of swagger blockers, come out as some mangled, beaten-up, affected version that people can easily misinterpret. If only our speech could come with little emojis for clarification.

As we grow up, we learn our vocabulary, rhythms, and speech patterns from our families. If our environment features easy-breezy language, we become relaxed. We might comfortably include sarcasm, humor, even profanity in our repertoire. Conversely, if the people around us are a little more rigid, that will creep into our patterns as well. Over time, and through exposure to new environments, the way we talk evolves and changes. University, work, partners, and friends will all play a role in shaping how we talk. In fact, our surroundings can have so much influence that we can even start to sound different just by hanging out somewhere new for a while. Do you think Madonna was born with that faux British accent? Nope. Hanging out in the UK and being married to a British guy was all it took to change the cadence and tone of her speech, but only because she chose to let it happen.

THE BULLSHIT OF "BUSINESS-SPEAK"

Something weird happens to us when we get out into the business world. We very quickly take on the "accent" of our workplace so that we can prove we're a legit member of the tribe. It happens to everyone, and it makes us feel damn good—like we belong and have earned a place among the other tribespeople.

This happened to me when I first started working in advertising. I was a copywriter in the newly formed digital division of the largest ad agency in Canada. The staff was composed of various tech freaks and geeks who were the pioneers of the industry. This was back in the day—a mere eight years after Netscape launched its first browser. The digital frontier was a mystery to most, and most definitely to me. But it was cool to be on the cutting edge.

I remember like it was yesterday. It was my very first team meeting, where everyone was sharing project updates and dealing with tech and creative issues. I think the only words I actually understood were "and," "but," and "website." For one of the first times in my life, I had no choice but to shut my mouth and listen. I scribbled down all the mysterious jargon, acronyms, and sundry unknown bits of language. Then I went on a mission to figure out what the hell they all meant. I wanted in on that tribe, big-time.

This was long before Google. If you wanted to get answers, you had to go on Yahoo! and the results were pretty slim. Of course, back then I was afraid to look like an idiot, so just straight-up asking people didn't feel like the best option. This was my first and biggest mistake. I spent the next few weeks drowning in a sea of insecurity and despair, terrified that I would be found out as the tech and advertising neophyte I actually was.

So I did what I could, constantly trying to put two and two together to make sense of terms and phrases. I started peppering my speech with the stuff I had decoded and felt so goddamn good when I used an acronym correctly. Once I felt that I had developed some cred, I would casually ask for clarification in a way that I thought wouldn't "out" me. With every passing day, I felt more and more like a digital badass. I mean, come on: I spoke the lingo! I was "one of them."

And then one night, I was at a family dinner. I was regaling everyone with my work stories, how I'd worked on this banner ad, that interstitial ad, written these CTAs, and that mouse type, and how the UX journey was driving consumer conversion (feel free to google all that)...

Suddenly my sister put her hand up. "OK," she said, "I have not understood a single word you've said in the last twenty minutes. Who are you and what the hell are you talking about?"

I laughed for a second and then stopped. Why was I feeling so thrilled about finally proving my belonging to one tribe while really not caring that I had alienated another? What *had* happened to me?

I had assimilated into the Borg, and I had the language to prove it. But in the process, I'd lost the real me. The way that I expressed myself had been sublimated by my desire to fit in. I had sold my words out for a place in the tribe—or, in plain old "Leslie-speak," I had disappeared up my own ass.

From that point on, I tried to just keep it real, to speak plainly and straight-up. Sure, clients loved it when I tossed their acronyms around like a tennis ball, because it made them feel like I was a part of *their* tribe. But I worked very hard to cut the bullshit and talk like a normal person as opposed to some advertising droid. Interestingly enough, it made me a far better copywriter because I always remembered to speak the language of real humans, not "consumers of marketing." And I like to think it made me a more interesting person.

FROM CLICHÉD TO CHARISMATIC IN JUST A FEW WORDS

This phenomenon is so common in the workplace that it features in every single one of my training sessions (plus every office-related satire on the planet), regardless of whether we're talking communication, leadership, storytelling, or creativity. It seems that most people have stopped being able to hear themselves. Their bullshit business-speak is so deeply embedded in their psyches that even when you point out that anyone who hadn't worked alongside of them for a decade would have no freakin' idea what they just said, they don't get it.

There's no such thing as "sounding smart."
To qualify as smart, you are either in a place of
knowledge or in a place of seeking it.

I've asked hundreds, maybe thousands of people why their speech has become riddled with business clichés, and what do you think the honest answer is? They think it makes them sound smart. That's what it all boils down to. They think that their language is proof of swagger. Forget that these are people with titles like SVP, VP, or even CEO: they're all equally worried about sounding smart. Hey, believe me, I get it. But I also get what a colossal waste of time it is.

There's no such thing as "sounding smart." To qualify as smart, you are either in a place of knowledge or in a place of seeking it. The former is about experience; the latter is about curiosity and openness. Sounding smart is about either or both insecurity and arrogance. These are the opposites of swagger.

Think about the people in your life whom you trust the most. The ones you go to for counsel, personally and/or professionally. The ones you want to be like when you grow up. Are they acronym-dropping automatons or are they warm, approachable, funny, and plain-speaking? Are you impressed by their ability to draw people in and engage them when they speak, regardless of whether it's one-on-one or in front of a room? And does it impress the shit out of you when they talk from a place of deep knowledge without being an arrogant asshole? They're more concerned with helping others understand the subject matter to the best of their ability than showing off what a rock star they think they are.

Yet, convincing people to drop their front and speak plainly in the business world is like pushing a boulder uphill. I have been told far too many times that this business-speak is "expected" of them and that people would judge them if they didn't use it. I don't buy it. I do buy that people believe it. But I don't buy that it's true for a second.

I was invited to speak at the "town hall" of a giant financial services organization. These sessions involve thousands of employees gathering in various locations to get updates from their big bosses on how business is progressing. When done badly, they're boring as hell—just a long-form lecture filled with all data and no insights. When done well, the sessions are part rallying cry, part motivational forum. (I get the feeling that most employees have come to expect the former.)

The senior VP took the stage. He was British, handsome, and totally energized. Reputationally, he was known to have moments of arrogance, to not always be the best listener, sometimes inaccessible, but also brilliant. He was considered a true innovator who had actively changed the company for the better, driven by pure, good intention, whom everyone wanted to work for regardless of his occasional leadership quirks. He was up there to close the show with a bang.

He started by saying, "I know I can be a real cranky-pants. I don't mean to be Mr. Cranky-Pants, but I know it can happen at times..."

With that one phrase, the energy in the room immediately shifted. Laughter rippled through the crowd and people shot each other glances and smiles. Bodies relaxed, along with the SVP's language. Then he made the rock 'n' roll sign of the horns, tossed out a few mild profanities, and joked around a little more, all of which had people laughing and sharing looks again. He was self-deprecating, warm, and honest. And when he was done, the room erupted in massive cheers.

Everyone broke for lunch, and I wandered around listening to people's comments. Over and over, I kept hearing how he had come across as "real" for the first time. How he seemed "so human." And how they loved it. His senior people commented that this was the most "himself" they'd ever seen. Real. Human. Himself. And all it took was "Mr. Cranky-Pants."

What had actually happened was that he had focused purely on them, not himself. He'd been more concerned about making his people feel comfortable than he was about impressing them or showing off. Ironically, by being both honest and a little vulnerable, he had impressed them more than he could ever have devised. And they loved him for it.

By bringing our true selves to light through our language, we open the channels of connection. And when our swagger can get out, appreciation and humanity can get in.

Laura, a development manager, told me the story of what happened after I'd challenged her constant use of business-speak whenever she was talking to somebody in a more senior position. My exact words to her were, "Cut the bullshit."

"It made me realize: Oh my God, I actually sound like this when I'm trying to have a regular conversation!" she said. "No wonder I was having a hard time connecting with these senior leaders and trying to get more out of my career—I sounded like a freakin' robot. But what I thought was 'proper mature business language' was actually alienating me from a genuine relationship with them. So, I just changed my choice of words. Now when I greet everyone—VPs, CIOs, it doesn't matter—it's literally, 'Hey, how are you?' Before, it would have been a formal 'good morning' or something. Even those kinds of changes have made a big difference. I've actually had feedback from leadership that I seem far more relaxed!"

Remember Morgan, the young bank AVP whom we met earlier? She had the issue in reverse, but the same result. As a new leader who was younger than her team, she had been using language to try and establish credibility. But when she dropped the front and started using her natural "millennial-speak," people warmed in response to her realness. "I *am* a millennial," she said, "so I'm going to speak like somebody who's my age, not someone who's sixty-five years old. And that's a good thing! I just talk like I do when I'm hanging out with family or friends. Yes, I keep it 'professional,' but it means I'm not putting on a mask when I walk into work."

**By bringing our true selves to light through
our language, we open the channels of connection.**

When we put tons of unnecessary mental energy into planning and second-guessing every word we say, it's unlikely that we're going to find our flow. But when we just let it rip, focus more on our truth and intention, what comes out of our mouths will find acceptance in ways we couldn't have imagined otherwise. Trust and believe. I know what I'm fucking talking about.

Which leads me to...

REASONS WHY SWEARING IS FUCKING AWESOME

Here's the quick-and-dirty on the use of expletives (pun intended). Authenticity, and all of its trappings, has gotten a bad rap. Some claim that it's simply an excuse to unmuzzle and spew whatever comes into one's head sans filter and without a care for the feelings of others. Ergo, those who readily and regularly include swearing in their convos are often criticized for using "authenticity" as a cover story for their lewd, crude, and rude communication choices. I mean, how could anyone not censor themselves out of respect for the delicate sensibilities of others?

I call major bullshit on that.

Anyone who knows me knows I'm a big fan of swearing. No, I don't do it to be shocking or to hurt others. And no, I don't suffer from a condition that prohibits me from self-censoring. I just really, really like it. It's honest, colorful, descriptive, emotive, provocative, and evocative—everything that language should be. It's also true to who I am and the intensity of what I feel, and a manifestation of my unadulterated joy in interacting with others. In other words, swearing is representative of my swagger. When I'm in my place of swagger, it means I'm bringing my full self to the party, and that's always good for business—both my own and those I work for and with. If I start censoring myself, who decides when, where, and how much? Therein lies a truly slippery slope for anyone.

Language is the expression of emotion. We use words to be emphatic or dramatic, to show how important something is or how much we've been affected by it. It has the power to carry our truth out into the world with gusto and cut through the noise, especially in the corporate world. It can prove that we really care about something and that we're willing to express it wholeheartedly and unequivocally. Of *course*, swearing factors into this!

Hopefully it goes without saying that using swearing as a weapon—aiming expletives at others—is totally unacceptable unless you're telling someone, "*You are so fucking awesome!*" In fact, you'll find that used in this way, most people are totally OK with it. Funny, that.

EVEN GOOD AND SMART HUMANS SWEAR

It's no secret that casual swearing can actually put people at ease. It signals that we're being informal and relaxed and thus more approachable and trustworthy. Haven't we all cracked a smile when a boss or someone we see as posh drops a casual curse world? "Human!" it screams to us. "Hallelujah. This person is actually *human!*" The tone is then set and the conversation usually gets more open and livelier. Remember how well it went for Mr. Cranky-Pants?

The equal appreciation of and controversy over swearing is so profound that countless studies have been done on the subject. According to a joint study by researchers from Maastricht University, Hong Kong University of Science and Technology, Stanford

University, and the University of Cambridge, those who swear like sailors are considered more sincere than those who don't indulge or who keep profanity to a minimum.

Need further proof of the trust thing? The study also mentions that, according to their state-level societal research, those societies that had the highest percentage of swearers also had a higher integrity score. And they were able to prove a "consistent positive relationship between profanity and honesty."[8]

Despite what you might have heard, swearing does not mean you're lazy, have a poorer vocabulary, or are less intelligent. Au fucking contraire. Apparently, if you want to show off your big brain, you should let your potty mouth fly. Cited in an article by Tommy Hawkins on the correlation between swearing and verbal intelligence, a 2015 study concluded that intelligent people tend to use more curse words. "Taboo or 'swear word' fluency is positively correlated with overall verbal fluency," Dr. Timothy Jay, co-author of the study, reported. "The more words you generated in one category meant the more words you generated in another category, orally and verbally."[9]

Try this test yourself.

> Time yourself to see how many swear words you can come up with in a minute. The greater the number, the higher your overall vocabulary is. Hell, why not go head-to-head with someone else? Make it a team contest. Rip the Band-Aid right off that taboo-boo!

And if you're still on the fence about swearing at work, even that has been proved as better than OK. A study published in the *Journal of Managerial Psychology* found that letting those curse words rip actually has positive benefits for staff morale.[10] Yup, this kicks the shit out of the traditional view that workplace swearing is a definite no-no. Oh—and folks would rather work at companies where culture accepts and includes a peppery dash of expletives.

DON'T JUST TOLERATE—CELEBRATE THE CUSS!

All this to say that speaking plainly and openly is cause for celebration, not censorship. Sure, it's good to get a sense of the tolerance of others. We don't want to actively offend. But if swearing is part of your truth, then know that it's OK to use it when and if necessary, and that being in the office doesn't mean limiting your word preferences. Like all language, it's a choice, and like all choices, you need to make it for yourself and take comfort in the knowledge that it doesn't make you a bad or "offensive" person.

For the record, I've found that most people have no problem with swearing when you do it to emphasize the positive or sympathize with the negative.

So, here's to expressing yourself with color, flavor, attitude, and unadulterated joy, however that may manifest. With your truth, intention, and self-belief in the driver's seat, you won't be talking out of your ass—it'll be straight from the heart.

17

FEELING YOUR SWAGGER

I CAN'T TELL you how many times people have told me that they're afraid of expressing their swagger lest they get labeled an "emotional wreck" or "unprofessional." Not surprisingly, this usually comes from women. But—and this may come as a surprise—not exclusively. Men are also concerned about expressing their emotions at work. And it's not just those in the trenches who are trepidatious. Everyone from interns to CEOs are cautious about having the "feels." So why have we been made to feel so shit-scared that proof of our complex humanity could minimize us in the eyes of our bosses, colleagues, or employees?

Because it's convenient. Emotions are messy. They can be hard to interpret and even harder to deal with for the inexperienced or unskilled. So establishing emotions at work as taboo makes it easier for everyone. But that's as realistic as a little kid standing in the corner covering their eyes and singing, "La la la, you can't see me!" because humans are as much made of emotion as they are of cognition. In fact, the two are inextricably intertwined and equally crucial in contributing to organizational culture.

All the wishing and hoping ain't gonna make emotions at work conveniently disappear. Every time we get criticized, rejected, admonished, or even celebrated, our brain's natural response will be emotional. Chemicals will be produced and reactions will ensue. Remember that our brains are wired to respond to danger. While we no longer have to fear the wooly mammoth trampling us to death, our brains now see cognitive threats as the enemy and produce the same powerful protective instincts. So we cry, shout, simmer, or rage in order to survive.

**All the wishing and hoping ain't gonna
make emotions at work conveniently disappear.**

Ironically, because men have long dominated the workforce, showing emotion has adapted to what would be typically seen as more male emotional responses, like yelling, pounding the table, or bullying. Somehow that's been deemed OK. But do the same as a woman and you're instantly labeled "a bitch," aggressive, or hard to manage. And shed a tear? Ohhh—now you're a lightweight, weak, and totally unprofessional. Sure, the stereotypes are changing, but not fast enough.

THE FACTS ON EMOTIONS AT WORK

Liane Davey, doctor of organizational psychology and *New York Times*–bestselling author of *You First* and *The Good Fight*, knows just about everything there is to know about dealing with emotions at work. Known as the "team doctor," she's educated and trained countless organizations on how to channel, harness, and use emotions effectively in the corporate environment. And she doesn't hold her own feelings back when addressing this often touchy subject. "Emotions aren't optional," she says. "As long as there will be human beings in the workplace, there will be emotion, period. We're uncomfortable with them because we like to be in control. By their very nature, emotional outbursts mean we're not in control."

She also expresses huge empathy for those who try to stifle their emotions at work because she knows it only serves to amplify them. By trying to squish them down, our bodies actually fight back so we can get them out of our systems. But once you become less afraid of expressing them, the need to express subsides.

"For example, I realized that every time I tried not to cry at work, I would literally shoot projectile tears," she told me. "But once I accepted that it was OK to cry in front of my boss, I cried way less often because I could find other outlets for my emotions. As soon as there was a safe place to express my emotions, then shit didn't have to squirt out of my face anymore."

But in a world filled with haters, judgment, and fear, how the hell do you establish that safe zone? The first step is recognizing what Liane calls "the injury." "What we need to understand in ourselves and others is the layer beneath the emotion—the values and beliefs that are being threatened," she says. "We mistake the emotional outburst as diagnostic when it's only symptomatic. So when strong emotions are being expressed, don't be distracted by it. Say, 'Oh—clue!' There's an injury happening here at the level of what matters most."

In swagger terms, the injury is akin to someone poking directly into your truth, intention, and self-belief. And we all know how much that stings. Of course, we're going to feel strongly about that, just as anyone would. So the resulting emotion is perfectly natural, only it's still scary as hell when you're in the middle of it. What to do next?

"It's OK to take a time out," she advises. "If you're, say, in the middle of a performance review that starts to get heavy, it's perfectly acceptable to say, 'You know what, I'm going to need a little break.' Then go and cry in the bathroom if you need to, and come back and say, 'OK, I'm ready now.'"

If you feel your eyes welling up, you can even own that shit. "Say, 'You know what, I feel like I'm going to cry right now, which isn't going to help the situation. I need to go so I can come back and have a better conversation.'" If you're worried about the stigma of confessing that tears are imminent, she recommends instead trying, "I can feel myself protecting against your feedback right now." Or, "I know I need to hear this. But right now, I feel like I'm shutting down. Can I come back to you on this shortly?"

This applies not only to bubbling tears but also to mounting frustration or anger. This type of response proves to your boss or colleague or whomever you're in the situation with is that while, yes, you are feeling stuff, you're not out of control. That makes them feel safer, which will result in them having more compassion for you. Knowing you have these escape routes can be critical in creating that safe zone that will help your threat response adjust going in.

As long as there will be human beings in the workplace, there will be emotion, period.

—DR. LIANE DAVEY

The key, Liane says, is to go *through* it. Not to stifle or suppress. Your truth will emerge somehow, somewhere, and it's better to continue moving forward in the hopes of addressing the underlying injury with those around you in a meaningful and productive manner. That way, they'll better understand and learn how to interact with you—and that's good for all concerned.

But what happens if you don't have the wherewithal to use your big-girl or big-boy words in the moment? You've ugly-cried all over your boss and are dreading the messy aftermath. Should you hand in your resignation? Take a few sick days to recover from the "embarrassment flu"? Or figure out how to throw yourself on your sword in front of them in dramatic hari-kari fashion? Nope. Not according to our resident expert.

"Don't apologize," Liane counsels. "Don't creep back in and start saying, 'I'm so sorry you had to see that.' What you want to do is thank them. Because you want to make it about *them*. Say, 'Thank you so much for being patient with me, or for caring enough about me to go through that messy bit. Thank you for asking the great questions or taking the time to get me into a more positive frame of mind.' Or even better, 'Thank you—you win the best [boss/colleague/team member] award for what a champion you were through that. You really helped me get to the other side of it.'"

The trick is to de-shame and de-stigmatize the whole event and reward the other party instead of begging forgiveness. This can actually help to change not only your relationships but also your culture through making those emotions positive for all.

THE UPSIDE OF EMOTIONS

Expressing emotions at work can also have countless other hidden upsides. Going through emotional events with others can cause the brain to release oxytocin, also known as the "cuddle" or "love" hormone, because it's also released when people snuggle up or bond socially. And we all know how damn good that feels. So being exposed and vulnerable can actually do the opposite of what we fear. Instead of being alienated, we're brought closer together as a tribe. When we've seen each other's hearts, we create empathy and tend to trust more.

**When we've seen each other's hearts,
we create empathy and tend to trust more.**

Remember that famous quote that goes, "They may forget what you said—but they will never forget how you made them feel"?[11] It's actually a scientific fact.[12] And it's a good reminder of how valuable emotion can be in being memorable, persuasive, and believable.

The extra cherry on the sundae is that the more you accept your own emotional realities and complexities, the more secure in your swagger you'll become. As a result, you'll be less hyperreactive to external triggers—your sense of self will strengthen and you'll be far less subject to what would have been injury before.

The more you accept your own emotional realities and complexities, the more secure in your swagger you'll become.

Perhaps most importantly, if you learn to be unafraid of revealing or expressing your emotions at work, you will be positively modeling what being a healthy human looks like, which can go an incredibly long way to healing negative culture. If people see you doing it and thriving, they'll be more likely to take the risk themselves. Before long, you'll see that you've contributed to better, stronger, and more swagger-y interactions with everyone. WOOT! Emotions for the win!

EVEN CEOS CRY

My favorite story of embracing one's own emotional complexity started with a creativity workshop I was delivering to an organization undergoing a big transformation. I asked key senior leaders to attend so that others could see that the top dogs were really serious about the change they were looking for. I'd met a few of the bigwigs but hadn't yet come face-to-face with the CEO.

It's important to know that despite the subject matter, this workshop requires real vulnerability and authenticity from participants. We ask everyone to post real-life problems to serve as subject matter for our creative problem-solving training. I make sure to clearly outline this and caution everyone that if their problem is chosen, they will have to discuss it among their smaller groups. Of course, they can choose to opt out, even at the last minute, if they decide that they're too uncomfortable to do it.

So I picked four problems to work on and read them out, asking for the problem owners to identify themselves. One by one, they raised their hands. The last hand raised belonged to a handsome, elegant, white-haired gent in the back of the room. "Would you be willing to work on your problem?" I asked, as I always do. In a British accent, the man said, yes, he would. And then we broke for lunch.

The person who had hired me for the workshop immediately rushed over and whispered, "That's Duncan, our CEO!"

"Hmm," I thought, "this could get interesting." During lunch, I sidled up to him. "I just wanted to double check with you on your comfort level," I said. "Shit's gonna get real up in here in a bit." He smiled a little nervously. "I'm going to try," he said. I told him he was brave and that what he was doing would be a real gift to the team.

After lunch, we reshuffled our groups and got down to work. Duncan's team was composed of participants from all levels of the company, from junior up. They quickly started investigating his problem, which turned out to be a symptom, not the root cause. The conversation became heavier and more intimate. As Duncan answered deeply personal questions about his life, his team leaned in, keenly intent on his every word. Inevitably (and as usual for this workshop), the emotions began to flow, and tears welled in Duncan's eyes. I casually walked over and watched, ready to intervene if necessary. With tears but seemingly without embarrassment, Duncan spoke his truth to his team, revealing himself to be, well, human. And you know what? His team cried right along with him.

At the end of the first day, with the emotionally challenging bit over and done with, I pulled him aside to ask how he was feeling. "It was amazing," he admitted. And in the words of a great leader, he said, "And I know it was great for the team."

But that wasn't the end of the transformation for Duncan. It's no surprise that we became fast friends after that. As I got to know him, I learned that as the regional CEO of a global company, and in a very male-dominated industry, he'd always felt very cautious about revealing his emotions. Despite being British and naturally averse to showing his feelings, he also feared it could be construed as weakness and could limit his chances of greater success.

But once the emotional horse is out of the barn, it's tough to put it back.

Cut to several months later. The company was having their global summit where regional CEOs and their employees from around the world got together to share successes, failures, and next steps. When Duncan took the stage to share his people's accomplishments, he suddenly found himself getting choked up. In the past, Duncan would have swallowed down the tears and gamely soldiered on. But this time, he decided to let them rip. Tears flowing freely, he spoke with pride about what his amazing team had accomplished and how he felt about it. When he was done, he received a standing ovation from the entire room.

**We fear that revealing our emotions
at work will impact our credibility,
when the opposite is true.**

In that moment, Duncan went from mere CEO to beloved badass leader. And it was the thing he feared most that allowed it to happen. In true swagger fashion, it shone a light on his incredible accomplishments, and even more importantly, showed all those dudes the kind of courage it took to get there.

So much of our fear around revealing our emotions at work is that we feel it will impact our credibility. Please know that it's just not true. And if you're working in a repressive and locked-up environment, you can either break out or break free. Being who you are deserves to be celebrated, not castigated. You have an opportunity to support other people's swagger journeys by bringing yours to light.

And for all of my sisters out there who wonder why the hell they can't help but shed a tear when they feel big feelings, you may be relieved to know that it's also biological. Women have six times more prolactin (the hormone related to crying) in their systems than men. Plus, we ladies contend with smaller tear ducts, so whereas a guy might "well up," women's tears course down their faces in dramatic fashion.

So next time someone gives you the side-eye for crying at work, simply tell them, "It's biology. Look it up," and then proudly walk your bad swagger-y self away.

PART FIVE

LIVING YOUR BEST SWAGGER LIFE

18

HOW DO YOU KNOW IF SWAGGER IS WORKING?

WE'VE LEARNED THAT living with swagger is a lifelong journey. It's kinda like working out. If you go to the gym every day, build up your cardio, and start getting those defined muscles (holy shit—I have *abs*!!), you can stop and celebrate—but as soon as you start sleeping in, missing workouts, and eating doughnuts for breakfast, you'll inevitably undo your hard work.

Swagger's no different. You gotta keep those psychological practices in play daily. And just like working out, there's no better incentive than recognizing when it's working and how far you've come. When you're getting fit, you can measure your results by number of pounds pumped, miles run, or inches lost. Swagger, on the other hand, can feel a little harder to quantify.

PROOF OF SWAGGER

Swagger doesn't happen in one fell swoop. While one badass act doesn't mean instant swagger, ten, twenty, fifty acts of authentic courage—now those start to add up. But we tend to look at our moments of swagger (and resulting positive responses to them) as one-offs or anomalies. We're freakin' stubborn creatures, and reprogramming our thinking can be a long and arduous process. So if we want to start believing that we're developing some real, consistent swagger, then we need a way to not just recognize the moments but also capture, reflect, and trust the memories of them. When something has been proved as true or real, it's harder for the brain to refute it.

YOUR PROOF OF SWAGGER CHECKLIST

While everyone will experience swagger in their own unique ways, I discovered that there are some very common proof points. Here's a handy ten-point Proof of Swagger checklist to make sure you don't miss out on a single point of validation! Use this as a starting place to make sure you're tracking and celebrating the changes that swagger brings.

1   You No Longer Bother Faking It

We know the old "fake it 'til you make it" advice goes against the swagger ethos. When you have swagger and don't have all the answers, you'll be the first to admit it. There will be no shame in it because you know that competence leads to confidence, not the other way around, and that the best way to up your game will be to raise your hand and ask for clarity. Swagger alleviates the fear of "looking stupid" simply because you'll know that you're not. You'd rather revel in curiosity rather than drown in ego.

2   You're No Longer Starving for Validation

People with true swagger don't give a rat's ass about whether others are judging them. They know their value in the world and don't require reminders. Instead of being driven by ambition, they're more concerned about being in their place of excellence. When someone celebrates your swagger, you're never self-deprecating. You take the compliment and appreciate it, but you don't *need* it. If you have swagger, instead of trying to get people to see that you're so awesome, you just get on with the job of being awesome and know your good work will get you the appropriate recognition in time.

3 Your Truth and Intention Are Always Clear

Those with swagger are genuinely interested in being of service to others and to the collective good. But they will not spout bullshit in order to achieve their own (or others') goals. When you have swagger, you feel compelled to speak your truth and always know why it's important to do so. You have a clear vision of what you need to say and do in order to make a difference, even if it's not popular. And somehow you manage to get away with it—much to the awe of your peers.

4 You Have Only One Face

People with swagger don't bother putting on a persona "mask." That means you're fundamentally the same in front of senior executives in high-stakes situations as you are with friends over beers. It doesn't mean that you don't get nervous, but you don't lose your mind (or your center) as a result. If you have swagger, people often admiringly say that with you, "what you see is what you get." You have a comfort in your skin that isn't shaken by circumstance.

5 You Have a Healthy Dose of "Don't Give a Shit-Ness"

Swagger doesn't walk around riddled with insecurity. While those around you are popping forehead veins due to career stress, your mind just doesn't go there. You're OK asking yourself, "What's the worst thing that could happen?" because you know the answer is "nothing that bad." Your perception of the world is pretty much aligned with reality, so you no longer sweat the imaginary stuff. And when life does throw you a challenge, you just step up with your truth, intention, and self-belief and hope for the best. Even at the worst of times, you are never reduced to being an asshole.

6 Your Generosity of Spirit Goes Off the Charts

When you have swagger, you become so OK with yourself that you have more energy and desire to help and support others. Whereas haters were once in your crosshairs, you now look upon them with sympathy, knowing they're lost in the swaggerless darkness. But because you no longer fear them, you now find yourself far more willing to extend a hand, even if they might initially try to bite it off. You know your swagger force field will protect you, so you can go and be a badass superhero who fights for good.

7   You Jump at Challenges

Present in front of a room of senior executives? Yes, please! Take the stage at a conference? Your hand shoots up. Take on a project that others have failed at? You've got this! Performance review? You literally sashay in. Go after a mentor you've only dreamed of? Hell, yeah. In fact, you believe that *you* might even have something juicy to offer *them*. When your swagger is in full bloom, the world starts to become a far more accessible and exciting place where challenges become opportunities. It's amazing how nimble one can be when the burden of self-doubt is lifted. So go dance in the forest, little swagger nymph.

8   You Stop Being a Robot

Because swagger requires you to dig deep into the real you, before long, all the shit that felt unnatural to you starts to fall away. Your language warms up; you're physically more relaxed; even your fashion sense may change now that you're OK with being perfectly imperfect and gloriously human. Anything forced or fake just feels wrong. You really notice when it's happened, and best of all, you know how to shift back to your true self in the moment.

9   You No Longer Beat Yourself Up

All those days of replaying situations after the fact and beating yourself up for what you should have but couldn't say or do at the time are gone. You've recorded over all of those old tapes and you're now 100% OK with your humanity. Sure, things won't always go as planned. And yes, there will be shit you don't see coming. But now you see them as learning opportunities as opposed to irrevocable disasters that can end you. Coming back at conversations you weren't happy with becomes easy, even (*gasp!*) enjoyable because it's yet another chance to prove to yourself what a swagger queen or king you've become. Farewell self-recrimination!

10 You're Just Plain *Happier*

Bounce in your step. Smile on your face. Love in your heart. It might sound sappy, but in my experience, people who've attained swagger nirvana are more energized, content, and stress-free. All that doom-and-gloom shit has been lifted. Now you know yourself and you *like* yourself. Hell, what's not to like? The side effect of this is that people will gravitate more to you, trust you, and ask for your counsel regularly. And no one with swagger ever gets picked last for dodgeball, even if they're the smallest or the slowest, because everyone knows they're going to be a total hoot when they play.

There are probably a hundred more indicators of swagger that I could list, some teeny, some huge. The most important thing to know is that after tapping into the real you, *you will feel different.* Guaranteed. Your swagger will be undeniable to you and those around you. Of course, you won't give a shit whether or not anyone else says it out loud. You'll just wake up and go to sleep knowing you're living your best life. Yaaasss, queens and kings!

PROOF OF SWAGGER MOMENTS

I asked people to share some swagger moments with me, and their responses varied from the minute to the mammoth, from the public to the private, and from the day-altering to life-changing.

Max told me, "I recently gave what I think was the best speech of my life. I felt like I actually showed up and wasn't beholden to anyone but myself, and for the first time, I felt comfortable in taking risks with my content. I talked about stuff I was deeply passionate about and was able to express how I thought the company was fucking up. I learned that my superpower is tied in large part to my emotive abilities."

Lydia's story was about driving forward an untested initiative: "Here I was, leading this little grassroots team that had put together a really innovative training program. I had to go into a senior executive meeting to pitch it and ask for a pretty penny. They all looked at me a little funny, and I could see that they weren't 100% sure. Then my SVP looked me straight in the eye and said, 'This had better work.' And I remember looking at him, having had very little interaction with him before, and saying, 'Of course this is going to work.' For me, that was a moment that's just stuck, and now there's no stopping me."

For Olga, swagger moments happen all the time. "Lately, if I am in doubt of something," she said, "I keep repeating to myself 'truth, intention, self-belief' and it really does work!"

Maria recalled a challenge thrown down by her CEO: "He wanted me to up the number of attendees for our big gala event. His exact words were, 'It's all in your hands, so don't fuck it up.' Uh, no pressure. Luckily, I'd built trust with the board, so I didn't need pre-approval for my choices. I found a bunch of ways to cut costs, so I didn't even have to ask for money. I called in favors, trusted my vision, believed in myself, and ended up putting on a kick-ass show that was essentially free! It was the best finale ever of our annual conference. I definitely felt my bad self for that one."

Adam recognized his growing swagger in retrospect. "At the end of the year, my family all wrote down things that we were the proudest of from the previous year," he said. "I wrote that it was recognizing more about who the 'true' me is and being comfortable in my own skin. This swagger journey has helped me to be confident in myself, not worry about others' perceptions, and to just be me. I've started letting go of those little voices of fear. I also know it goes even deeper than this, because I can feel a change in my core. This recognition is very liberating."

Tenley's swagger moment was literally life-changing. "I asked my VP to meet to discuss my career next steps," she told me. "He'd been a big supporter of mine, and I decided it was time to cash in my swagger chips. I sat him down and said, 'Hey, you've seen me in my career thus far, and I'm at the point where I'm looking for a change in my future.' And he said, 'OK, what's your criteria?' So I told him straight-up. I asked to stay living in one city but have a team in our head office location in another—and I wanted him to pay for all of the related travel that would be required. He looked at me and asked, 'Really?' 'Yeah,' I said, 'because I'm worth it, and you know it.' His response? 'Yeah, that's true.' I'd always thought it, but I never had the guts to say it out loud. But now, I know that I'm worth celebrating."

Initially, Dan tried to avoid his swagger moment because he couldn't see it coming and had no idea how it would alter the trajectory of his life. "I was working at my ad agency and they were trying to get younger leadership to speak at the South by Southwest conference. They asked me to submit a proposal, but I immediately said no. I mean, speaking's not really my thing. The day the proposals were due, a mentor of mine asked how my submission went. I said, 'Uh, I didn't actually submit.' He looked at me for a second with that disappointed dad look and said, 'Oh. I see.' I slunk away and thought, 'Oh my God, I really disappointed him.' Now it wasn't really about me. So I quickly put together something and emailed it to the conference. I got shortlisted and ultimately chosen to speak out of over 3,300 entrants."

But that wasn't even the real swagger moment. When Dan was in the middle of delivering his speech to a packed room, the fire alarms suddenly went off… and kept going off. That would have rattled even the most experienced speaker, but Dan just treated it as a comedy improv moment, the very topic of his speech, and showed the audience how to keep it real and go with the funny flow through any situation. And it worked. Dan's session received the highest audience marks possible for both content and speaker.

"If you're not authentic," he said, "then you can't actually connect with people because it's your persona that's trying to make the connection, not you. But when you surface your real self, your true swagger, then connection becomes so possible and powerful. You can make people laugh, make them feel better, and even inspire them. I've seen that if you're vulnerable and open to it, even in front of two hundred people, people are very accepting of you. The real you."

Not long after, Dan left his agency job to pursue life as an entrepreneur. He created a game, was chosen to be on the TV show *Shark Tank*, and, yes, you guessed it, received funding from the Sharks themselves.

"I learned that it's about taking what you believe you deserve," he said. "If you don't decide what you want, the world will definitely decide for you. This is me—the one version of me."

And then there's Dahlia, whose swagger moment came in the form of something small, almost everyday, but for whom it was the arrival of a lifelong endeavor.

**A swagger moment can be the smallest thing,
but it really can change your whole life.**

—DAHLIA

"I've been out and proud as queer for over twenty-five years," she told me. "It had never been a problem for my career or anything, but there was a part of me that was still hiding. I'd always been a little insecure about how I looked. I could see the other women around me, and I knew I didn't fit into the typical mold of 'feminine.' But I always believed I had to look a certain way, to appear more 'girly' in order to fit in. I didn't feel comfortable wearing high heels or dresses, and I realized that I was still hiding behind a certain physical persona."

While she was very successful, there was that little voice inside her that was telling her she had to fit in with a more traditional female archetype in order to be successful. "I'd be in a client meeting and smart things would be coming out of my mouth, but I'd suddenly get really worried that the CEO at the table, male, or even female, who was dressed in a traditional business suit, would look over at me and think, 'I don't really get her; I can't connect with her.' Incredibly, I found myself playing the game in order to fit in, and then on the other side of that feeling unbelievably insecure because I wasn't myself. And that was not swagger-y at all."

Dahlia's secret "girly" weapon was her long, lush hair. She could wear it loose and flowing to up her "chick factor" or put it in a bun to come across as more "professional." One day, she decided that the cost to her self-confidence wasn't worth it. "I decided to cut off all of my hair," she says. "But I was really scared. I was worried that it could change the course of my professional life. Maybe I would no longer be considered for the managing director role I was up for. Or I wouldn't look the part or fit into that leadership team. Would they want to put me on their website if I looked like this?" she asked herself. "Then I just said, 'Fuck it, I'm doing it.'"

Dahlia razed off her waist-length hair in favor of a full pompadour, shaven sides and all. It was what she called "a typical men's cut." And it was an epic move.

"I can safely say it changed my life," she told me. "I gave myself permission to look a certain way, and it felt so good because I looked like myself! At forty-seven years old, I could finally look in the mirror and see the real me. It also allowed me to finally be a confident human being. So, if you weren't going to give me a job because of my haircut, it was just silly, because not only were the things coming out of my mouth still smart, I was now a better, more confident person."

And what about that promotion she was so concerned about?

"I got that promotion," she reported. "I was made managing director of my division, went to conferences, to New York to meet with the holding company. Nothing bad happened. And nothing stood in my way. I think we do a lot of work to make sure that people are OK with us," she said. "But I think that's really detrimental to not only our swagger and self-worth, but also how we function in the world when we don't show up as ourselves. A swagger moment can be the smallest thing, but it really can change your whole life. It changes everything."

Small, medium, or mega, each swagger moment we have matters and counts. The key is to never disregard even the teeniest act of badassery. If we've consciously established our truth, intention, and self-belief in advance of *any* situation and are able to act on it—even in the tiniest way—that's an amazing *win*! I promise you that those moments will add up and, before you know it, you'll have more consistent, more conditioned reactions to whatever life throws at you. Because swagger is not just about what you do, it's also about how you *feel* about what you do. One person's casual comment can be another person's moment of utter courage, and no one gets to decide that but you.

> 66
> **Swagger becomes part of your essence,
> your "being." Now it's just who I am.**
> —TENLEY

Keep in mind that part of living with swagger is learning to be OK with being seen in all of your perfectly flawed glory. That means that people may still see you in moments of anger, frustration, sadness, indecision, and failure. It's the fact that you're not afraid to hide these things that matters. The secret all humans share is that we all crave to be truly seen and accepted for who we are. The inability to achieve that goal comes when we don't have the courage to actually let others see the things we want them to accept. This makes us lonely, disenfranchised, and downright sad. While there are so, so many amazing reasons to seek swagger, I think that it first and foremost requires us to be seen, and that is the single greatest benefit. All of the other stuff is just the really fucking delicious icing on your soul cake. Tenley said it best: "I just don't need validation anymore. That's definitely what swagger has given me. It becomes part of your essence, your 'being.' Now it's just who I am."

SHOUTING OUT YOUR PROOF OF SWAGGER MOMENTS

The faster we can move from thought to action with swagger, the faster it will cement. We don't want to have to continually question whether truth, intention, and self-belief are worth it or whether or not we're actually building swagger. We want and deserve proof.

Now I want you to go a little public with your swagger. This will help you own that shit. And you need to own it big-time.

So, let's imagine you did something that was powerful and real at the same time. It doesn't matter how epic or tiny the task was. I don't care if it was the way you signed off an email or if you had a sales call during which you spoke your truth about your value. It could have been walking up to someone at a networking event and coming up with a completely "you" opening line. Or it could have been saying no to something you just knew wasn't right for you. Each of those, as an example, qualify *large* as swagger moments.

Here's what I want you to do.

1 Make sure that you've faced down the Negative Automatic Thought (NAT) and are deep in your Positive Automatic Thought (PAT).

2 Ask yourself, "What just happened?"

3 Answer it. For example, "I just killed an opening line at this networking event!" Take a second. Feel it.

4 Now capture it somewhere. Whip out your phone, dictate it, record a little video, or jot down some notes. And make sure you don't capture only the action, but also what reaction there was to it and how it made you feel. So: "I just killed an opening line at this networking event. Even though my heart was pounding a little, it actually felt totally natural coming out of my mouth. The guy smiled and laughed and shook my hand. And then we had a great chat. I felt relaxed, myself, and more than a little proud."

Awesome.

Now here comes the hard part. Share the moment—authentically. Whether you tell someone, post it on social media, or write a blog post about it, it doesn't matter. This is how you can own it. If you get it out of your head and heart, it's easier to examine it. It also starts to add up as a chronicle of sorts. If you're sharing your swagger moments with your best friend, colleague, or partner, every once in a while, you can ask them to reflect back some of the ones they thought were particularly cool.

Or just use the hashtag #SwaggerMoment and share it on social media: "Just pulled out the most 'me' opening line ever at a networking event. Worked big-time! #Swagger-Moment." It won't take long before your feed becomes an irrefutable timeline of your developing confidence. And because it's honest and you and not bullshit, you're totally allowed to share it.

Remember, swagger is more about self-acceptance than it is about self-assuredness. So if you worry about what other people might think, it defeats the whole purpose. Besides, fuck 'em if they can't handle a little self-congratulation.

My one piece of advice here: don't turn this into an opportunity to "humble brag," like, "I just won the Entrepreneur of the Year award. Why they would *ever* pick me is a mystery. What were they *thinking*?" Puke. Not only is that so inauthentic it makes my eyeballs throb, it's also self-deprecating, which is actively taking something away from yourself. Don't do it. The world will try and take us down enough on its own. Don't help it. Own your swagger. Speak your truth. Celebrate your intention. Revel in your self-belief. Remember, competence breeds confidence. Capturing and sharing your swagger moments will be your reminder that you're building competence little by little, step by step.

So here's your challenge *right now*.

Pull out your phone. Record your last swagger moment in writing, audio, or video. Now share it. Send an email; make a call; post on Facebook, Twitter, or Instagram—#SwaggerMoment.

Be undeniable. Make your swagger a fact.

19

LEARNING TO SWAGGER WHILE EVERYONE IS WATCHING

BASED ON JUST about everyone I interviewed for this book, and on what I've seen out in the proverbial field, swagger makes a person not just feel but also *seem* different. If they're used to you staying quiet, taking shit from people, questioning your decisions, or asking for validation, when you stop, it may come as a surprise or even a shock to others. While that's really cool and reassuring when your swagger is in full flight, it may not be wonderful to know that eyes are upon you while you experiment, fail, and try again.

Have you ever told anyone that you were on a diet or trying to give up drinking, and then the next time they saw you reach for a cookie or give in to a glass of bubbly, they gave you the side-eye or a blatant, "Hey, I thought you were off that stuff"? We all know how crappy *that* feels. Your swagger journey may fill others with awe or envy because they're still firmly stuck in their swagger blockers. Or you may even be on the receiving end of anger that they'll no longer be able to control or manipulate you. And there's nothing that those assholes like more than watching you try and fail. They may even try to contribute to your downfall. But more on that later.

The point is that it can be really tough to change while others are watching you. And they will be watching.

Because the confidence that swagger brings is such a sought-after commodity, it has a way of shining like a beacon. We've learned that once you have swagger, you'll develop a kind of magnetic force that draws people to you. They'll want to bask in your bravery, align themselves with your newfound power, and even try to absorb some of your self-belief. This means they will lean in and take note. But being under a microscope can in and of itself cause your confidence to fail you when you need it most. If you've spoken your truth at five meetings in a row, all heads may swivel in your direction in the sixth meeting when a contentious issue is raised. Half of the room is praying you'll let rip, while the other half may be silently hoping you keep shtum. You end up a little damned if you do and damned if you don't.

And change is equally tough on the inside. Like learning anything new, you may question your choices or decisions. Swagger novices have reported lying in bed awake at night agonizing over whether speaking their truth or changing their behavior is going to come crashing down on them. Perfectly normal. No new skill is cemented overnight; thus, the associated confidence takes time. Remember that it is competence that breeds confidence, not the other way around. But you can still choose how you feel about the process. There's a big difference between self-reflection and self-doubt. So sure, run the scenarios back through your mind. But instead of second-guessing yourself, look for the moments, actions, or reactions that fuel and reinforce your swagger.

However much we think we'd like to, we can't read other people's minds, so we don't actually know for sure how they feel about what we say or do. Hell, even if they *tell* us, we can't always trust it—unless we have a deep connection with them. The only reliable source is *you*. Look for points of differentiation, even if it's just the new thoughts or feelings that were in your head. Maybe you outed them with grace; maybe you planned well in your mind but weren't able to execute just then. That's called progress, and only *you* need to know that. Change will happen on the inside and leak out over time. But swagger means you don't need external validation anymore, right?

So if someone asks you, "Why didn't you say something?" you can reply with a casual, "I wanted to better understand my intention before I got into it." That should floor them. "Intention?" they may think. "What the fuck does that even mean?" Just smile enigmatically. Because you'll know *exactly* what it means.

Part of what you're doing while you evolve is modeling it for oth-

**Once you have swagger, you'll develop
a kind of magnetic force that draws people to you.**

ers. Wouldn't it be an incredible world if *everyone* had swagger? Your journey makes you a swagger ambassador of sorts. If you want to feel super-badass, think of yourself as the Swagger Gandhi who is "being the change you want to see in the world." Don't be afraid to talk about it. Share what you've learned and how it's affecting you. That's your truth, too. Part of that is modeling how to handle failure or disappointment.

So if your swagger receives a beatdown in a public forum, show the world how you can contextualize the experience appropriately as a wobble, not a decimation. Nothing will boost your heart and soul like a "you handled that really well" comment, especially when the same scenario would have had you crying in the bathroom in your pre-swagger days. (For the record, crying in the bathroom is still completely OK. That's a release, not a failure.)

Offer to help and support others. I've noticed that those who've embraced swagger often experience a deluge of requests to become mentors or advisors. Duh! Of *course* they do. People *want* to live authentic lives. They just don't always know how. Being in a swagger leadership position allows you to openly share what you've learned and be totally honest about what you've been through for good and bad. That's such a freakin' gift you can give to the world!

Your swagger is for you. The by-product is awesome for the world. But you're doing it for the betterment and happiness of only you first. So shed those pounds of insecurity, put down the bottle filled with fear, and dance that change like nobody is watching.

20

LOVING THE SWAGGER HATERS

BEING IN THE swagger zone can feel like a double-edged sword at times. On the upside, you walk around feeling like your bad self, experiencing massive boosts of confidence, and you have far more time and energy for what's important. The downside is that it can make people really uncomfortable because it shines a light on their own issues. Why should you feel so great when they still feel crappy about themselves? Just like schoolyard bullies, their instinct is to try and take you down a notch so you can wallow in the crap along with them. What they don't know is that while swagger may ferret out the haters, it also gives you the power to rise above with strength, self-assuredness, and even a sense of humor.

DEALING WITH SWAGGER HATERS

Meghan, a rising star in the corporate world, told me she has seen an increase of swagger hating as she continues to achieve. "I get told I'm aggressive a lot—often as a very detrimental statement," she said. "But you've got to go back to your swagger questions: 'Why am

I saying what I am saying? What is my truth, intention, and self-belief?' And then ask, 'Is that just a judgment of me or is that actually what I'm trying to do?' And if it's about what I'm trying to do, that's OK. You have to remind yourself: 'I am who I am, and I believe in something, and I'm just not going to let this external shit get in the way of that.'

> 66
>
> **When people see you hitting your stride, knowing and loving yourself, that's *exactly* why they come for you. Because you've found something they haven't yet. You've just got to deal with these fuckers.**
>
> —MEGHAN

"I think when you're finding your swagger, that's when those people come out the most, which is all the more reason why you have to be comfortable with who you are, and know how to shut it down." Meghan adds, "When people see you hitting your stride, knowing and loving yourself, that's *exactly* why they're coming for you. You just have to roll with it. Because you've found something they haven't yet. You've just got to deal with these fuckers."

There's nothing swagger haters despise more than an unshakable sense of self. It truly pisses them off. Especially when the old shit that used to work on you has no effect anymore. That's part of the fun of finding your swagger. You discover a whole new toolkit to handle their vitriol. And, boy, does that ever make you feel like a badass.

Lita, an IT project manager, told me, "Now that I have slingshot myself into my future, the haters really show themselves. Before, I knew there was something underlying, and I wondered, 'Do they not like me?' or, 'Did I say something wrong?' But now that I've come out the other side with my swagger and I know that my intent is pure, that my direction is set, and that I'm confident and comfortable in myself, I see them for what they are.

"A guy at work recently asked me who my sugar daddy was from a career perspective because I was getting some opportunities that other people weren't. Honestly, a year ago I would've gone into the washroom to cry or grabbed my stuff and gone home because I wouldn't have been able to be face him for the rest of the day. I'd have taken it so personally, like, 'What did I do to make somebody else think that I've done something wrong or illicit to get an opportunity?' It would have hurt me so badly. But this time, I just punched the guy in the arm and said, 'Oh my God, that's so cute. You're jealous.' That's what swagger does for you."

Score: 1 for swagger, and 0 for the haters!!

THE SECRET GIFT OF SWAGGER HATERS

I've learned that no one is immune to haters. It doesn't matter what your level, title, or accomplishments are. In fact, it's the very opposite. The higher you rise, the more the trolls sit below you and stare up, trying to figure out how to saw the legs off the magical ladder you seem to be climbing.

And they're such dumbasses; they rarely consider the fact that you might be able to knock them out with a single blow. In Jennifer's case, this is meant literally.

At only thirty-five years old, Jennifer Huggins has an incredible list of achievements to her name. She's a successful entrepreneur who owns her own boxing gym where she trains and coaches. She's the founder of the Fight to End Cancer charity that's raised millions, and an international three-star boxing referee and judge who does qualifiers for the Olympic Games. She's an official for the International Boxing Association, the newly elected president and chief official of her region's boxing association, and, in her spare time (eye roll), she's also a magician's assistant who travels the world performing to sellout crowds.

A résumé like this is guaranteed to have the haters lining up.

"So many of the people who helped me get to where I was turned around and tried to tear down the things I'd accomplished," she told me. "I've been on the receiving end of tons of personal attacks. You know, I'd have to sleep with a hell of a lot of people to have ever achieved the things that people say I have by doing just that. I mean, gosh, in the number of industries that I'm in, I would have been one busy girl—and I'm already pretty busy!" she says with a laugh. "Or luck. That's another one. People try to minimize what I've done by putting it down to some kind of good fortune. Except I spend every day looking at the things that I'm doing and making sure that they're in line, just so that I can prepare for the worst-case scenarios—every single day. So it's not luck, or sexual activity, or gender that's driving the success. It's none of those things."

At the level Jennifer is operating, the swagger hating can manifest in extreme ways, beyond what most of us have ever had to deal with.

During qualifiers for the 2016 Rio Olympics, she found herself smack in the middle of a corruption scandal that rocked the boxing world. Alone in a foreign country, and the only female official on the road, Jennifer learned just how serious haters could be.

"The people asking me to engage in dishonest activities were as much pawns as they were trying to make me be," she said. "They told me that I was a stupid girl who would never be assigned to these competitions again if I didn't listen to the things they were telling me to do."

But Jennifer is someone who lives by her truth, intention, and self-belief. Despite what was very real danger, she chose not to give in. "Looking back, I could very well have been injured or killed," she said. "The stakes were incredibly high for these people who would tell me, 'You need us in order to be in the position you're in.' And if that's true, you know what? I don't want that position."

So what's Jennifer's approach on dealing with haters big and small?

"A mentor of mine taught me a great rule to live by: it's called 3-4-3. You need three people in your life who are gonna totally hate you, who are toxic and will try and take you down. Then you need four people who just don't give a shit one way or the other. They'll just stand by, do their own thing, and not express any opinion on what you're doing. Lastly, you need three people who are gonna totally put you on a pedestal, lift you up—and in their eyes, you can do no wrong. Because these 3-4-3 represent the greater world.

You need them to stay in balance. I've learned to embrace the haters, the stupid shit they say, and recognize that it's on them, not on me. But without them, I might not check myself regularly. I've also embraced the 'neutral,' because they give me the space I need from all the other noise. And the people who love me? Well, it's great for reassurance, but they can also be distracting from your ultimate goals because they encourage you to settle for where you are."

As someone who relies on her swagger on a daily basis, Jennifer's advice on staying in a place of truth, intention, and self-belief is deceptively straight-up—but deep as hell. "Make your decisions simple," she says. "Ask, 'Can I live with myself today? Can I die with myself today?' I think we tend to make decisions thinking we're going to benefit from them sometime in the future. But really, we don't know how long we've got. So make your intention right for right now."

LEARNING TO LOVE YOUR HATERS

Nkechi is another great example of how ridiculous haters can be and how freakin' stymied they are in the face of immovable self-belief. She's the founder and CEO of Empowered in My Skin, an organization that aims to help people around the globe live purposefully in the comfort of their own skin. She's also a successful technology executive who leads teams on major tech implementations. And believe it or not, Nkechi is hated for her unending positivity.

"Someone on my team came to me and told me, 'People are talking about how they're disturbed by your positivity. They feel it overshadows the opportunity for them to open up to you about their areas of concern because they think you only want to hear the positive.' And then the conversation turned into whether or not I'm fake, if I'm keeping it real or just trying to impress. It led me to ask myself if I was manifesting my authenticity the way I wanted to, which is always a great learning experience for me."

But like Jennifer, Nkechi has learned how to not only rise above but also appreciate the negativity in her life and use it productively. She said, "I told her that I think it's important to have haters because they teach you how much you're stretching yourself, whether you're going all in, and digging in the spaces other people wouldn't dare to go. Haters offer a level of tension that you need to know if you're playing small or playing big."

So how did Nkechi handle her haters? "We have a team call every Friday where everyone gets to share what they've done that week," she said. "I kicked it off by sharing what I'd heard and how it had taught me a lot about who I am. Then I clearly told them they can come and talk to me about absolutely anything regardless of how ugly or bad it might be. I explained that when they walk into my space, I don't care how they come in—frustrated, angry, dejected. I'm going to give them two ears, close my mouth, and listen with empathy. And I promised them that when they left, they would feel better than when they came in.

"Listen," she told me, "100%, haters are needed because I think they open up avenues for you to explore and grow more. It's just a reminder that you're stepping outside of the box of what is common. Because haters don't hate on common people."

Truer words were never spoken.

Look, it's never fun when people have a go at you, whether it's a side-eye, a major callout in a public setting, or a subtle takedown during a private one-on-one meeting. And it may still hurt. You're human. But swagger is like a Star Trek force field around your true self that repels negativity and judgment and keeps it from penetrating your energy core.

So when the swagger haters come, it's up to you to make the decision about how much importance you want to give them. You can simply brush them off, or you can hold them at arm's length and examine them like a specimen. Is whatever they say worth considering or is it so much bullshit? If you notice it trying to worm into your center and corrode your truth, intention, and self-belief, it's critical that you take a step back and figure out which of your swagger blockers it's getting its power from. Is it penetrating your ambition and making you want to please people in the hopes of maintaining your status? Or is it wriggling through your insecurity layer and causing you to wonder whether their opinion of you is more correct than your deep understanding of yourself? (Not bloody likely, by the way.)

Above all, if you find yourself impacted by haters, you need to recognize that in the moment, like a giant light bulb going on. Stop. Take a deep breath and leave your body for a second. Imagine yourself hovering above the situation as an objective observer. The exact language I use while I'm doing this assessment is, "Isn't it interesting that..." This allows me to not feel the pain of it while it's happening, because pain isn't necessarily the right or even required response. But we're so conditioned to the *oof* of the gut punch that haters are trying to land, we think we need to feel it first. That's the memory of pain talking. What swagger gives you is the ability to stay objective and really question what's happening, or, as we've learned from some of our swagger queens and kings, to actively embrace that shit to help us have perspective and grow from it.

Criticism and judgment is about *them*, not about you. Remember that it's a freakin' *opinion*, and for every hateful one, you'll find a positive one to counteract it. We've learned that being bland and banal may keep the haters quiet, but it's also an indicator that we're not living up to our full potential. Having your swagger turned up full blast is like cookies for cockroaches.

CLOSING THE POWER BUFFET

So, I've saved one of my best secrets for last. It's one of the greatest "fuck you" truths of all time, and it is your secret weapon in the war against swagger haters. It is this: *No one can take your power.* It's just not possible. You can choose to give it to them willingly, but they cannot take it without your permission.

When you have swagger, it's like being in possession of the most epic buffet possible. Laden with delicious treats, exotic tidbits, steaming heaps of filling comfort food, and lots and lots of chocolate desserts.

When the haters encounter you, they're gonna gaze upon the bounty, smell that irresistible aroma, and do anything to get some of what you have. And they are always hungry as fuck.

Having your swagger turned up full blast is like cookies for cockroaches.

If you let them, they'll come snacking. They'll grab those giant plates and start filling them up—a little bite here, a nibble there. Some of them will see it as an all-you-can-eat chow-down. You have the choice to *let* them step up and start to feast, or you can take a big step back, smile, and announce, "The buffet is closed." Down come the steel shutters. Sure, they'll howl and complain. Who wouldn't? You're freakin' delicious. You're sustenance! Your very essence is the life force that keeps their assholery alive and kicking. But they don't deserve a single freakin' morsel.

Swagger is power. Don't you forget it. The haters may want to eat it for breakfast, lunch, and dinner, but you're the only one with

Haters don't hate on common people.
—NKECHI

the keys to the shutters. Seeing swagger haters for who and what they are is beyond liberating. And we all need tools, techniques, and tricks to keep them at bay. Some learn to embrace them, some use them as a balanced scorecard, and others just walk away. However you choose to deal with them, just know that they can say and do whatever the hell they want, but *they cannot take your power*. You've worked way too hard for that shit to just give it away.

Sorry, haters, the buffet is now closed due to an abundance of swagger.

21

WHEN SWAGGER SLIPS

SHIT HAPPENS—EVEN TO the swagger-filled. Life has a magical way of coming at you with unimaginable crap. You know, the stuff you just cannot really prepare yourself for. It might be a sprinkle or a fucking tsunami, but inevitably, shit will happen to all of us. I know that swagger is supposed to be the ability to manifest the real you in the face of all the psychological crap that's going to come for you, regardless of the situation or environment. And while that's perfect-world swagger, sometimes what comes at you or for you will cause your swagger to wobble, weaken, or completely fall away.

But that doesn't mean it's gone for good. Knowing that can be a lifeline when you're drowning in a sea of pain or self-doubt. I know this to be absolutely true, because it happened to me.

My mom passed away recently after a fierce battle with cancer. When she died, she created a giant black hole in my world, which completely sucked my swagger into its vortex. I quickly realized that her passing had fundamentally changed me. Nothing felt right, comfortable, or familiar. The sound of my own voice felt wrong in my ears. My creativity bailed on me, taking my confidence with it. What was left felt like a brick in the space where my heart had been.

As someone who had always relied on my incredibly strong sense of self to bail me out of tough situations (in large part because of what my mom had taught me), I was shocked to discover that I had lost it—my core, my center. The very definition of swagger was gone.

And to make matters worse, it up and left me smack-dab in the

**Sometimes life will cause your swagger
to wobble, weaken, or completely fall away.
But that doesn't mean it's gone for good.**

middle of writing this very book. So how the hell could I be the "swagger pied piper" if I was altogether directionless? I gotta tell you, it was pretty fucking scary.

For me, it was due to a death. But loss of swagger can result from myriad situations—getting fired, a breakup, a harsh critique at work, learning that someone you trusted wasn't trustworthy after all, gaining weight, losing weight, losing a friend or a beloved boss. It can happen when we backslide, lose traction, fall from grace, or simply fall apart. There are *so* many scenarios that will come for your swagger.

So, what can you do when you realize that, despite your best efforts, your swagger isn't where you left it?

Don't fake it. Pretending that all is perfect with the world feeds directly into developing a false persona, which, ironically, is one of the top swagger blockers. If you're feeling shitty, empty, insecure, or just plain sad, say it out loud. There's no faster way to discover who actually cares about you than when you honestly answer the question, "How are you?" Tell people what's going on, how you feel. Remember that being seen is part of the swagger game. You don't need to share the "why" if the details are a little too gory, but you sure can express the "what." After all, it's your truth, and speaking it can really help you find your way back to your swagger source. (PS: If people can't handle your truth, they're not your people.)

Lie low. Sometimes swagger piggybacks on energy. If you're emotionally or physically depleted, swagger can be tough to manifest. So protect your space and time for a little while. Say no to anything you really don't want to do. Avoid swagger-suckers and haters. Stay off social media. Now is not the time to be comparing yourself to the false image of perfection you'll find there. Relax and be kind to yourself. If that means pj's, Netflix, wine, and popcorn, so be it. It's only temporary.

Revisit something you're good at. Reminding yourself that you're a well-rounded and complex human can do wonders for your swagger. If there was something you had a gift or talent for at some point in your life, but you haven't had or made time for it of late, try to get back into it. It doesn't have to be hard-core. Go sing some karaoke. Take a one-off painting class. Go back to a gym class you once liked. Write a blog post. Just find one thing that used to make you feel happy and revisit it. Sometimes a little spark is all you need to reignite your swagger fire.

Help someone else. Compassion is badass, regardless of whether it's for ourselves or others. When we feel truly shitty, discovering that we still have the capacity to help other people can do wonders to pump up our confidence. Offer to mentor someone at work. Do a little volunteering. Or just reach out to help a friend. It will remind you of what you're still capable of. Besides, being of service is actually good for you. This is the focus of fifty scientific studies funded by The Institute for Research on Unlimited Love (yep, that's a real thing), which discovered myriad health benefits of doing good for others, including the overproduction of feel-good brain chemicals like dopamine and oxytocin.[13] So when your swagger is low, you can still be high on love!

Face down a demon. Have you been avoiding dealing with a person or situation? Whether it's a colleague who keeps claiming credit for your ideas, an asshole boss who refuses to acknowledge your accomplishments, or a friend whom you feel has been taking advantage of you, now could be a good time to right those wrongs. Plan your attack carefully. Don't engage until your emotions are firmly in check. Always keep your truth, intention, and self-belief firmly in mind, which will likely be tough given your state of heart and mind. Make sure you have contingencies in place should your initial approach turn to shit. And then go and get it done. Be direct, firm, and honest, and do not let anyone turn the tables on you. When you're done, you'll feel so much better and the future will look so much brighter.

Embrace your superpower. Every single one of us has something special and magical to offer. It could be our empathy, creativity, strength, insight, or ability to get people talking or put others at ease. Some of us are super-practical, can fix anything, or are amazing problem-solvers. Take some time to reflect and remember what makes you special, and then dive back into that. What helped me get a swagger refill after my mom's passing was getting back in front of people in training rooms (when I felt ready). The act of using my superpowers to fill up other humans reminded me of my purpose and power. It was like refueling my swagger source.

Remember, it's only temporary. Once a swagger-y badass, always a badass. Although the world may have knocked you around a bit, this too shall pass. Remind yourself that you are not your feelings. Consciously separating yourself from them helps immensely. Try saying, "I feel shitty" as opposed to "I am shitty." Those emotions will ebb and flow and fade, and the gorgeous, amazing, badass you are will still be standing at the end, proudly waving your freak flag. And your swagger will be even stronger for the experience.

Call on your champions. You know those people who always have a kind word, who celebrate you even when you can't celebrate yourself, who would happily make voodoo dolls to take down your haters? Yeah—those awesome people. Now's the time to go to them for help. It might sound totally weird, especially if you're uncomfortable with praise, but ask them to remind you of why they think you're awesome. They'll be more than happy to tell you. Hell, they've been telling you all along. Despite feeling crappy, don't argue or dispute their accolades. Drink it up like a long cool lemonade. Take a freakin' bath in it. Roll around like a pig in it. They'll remind you that you are not done—your awesomeness is just hibernating, preparing to emerge when the psychological climate warms up a little. You'd do the same for them.

Make no sudden movements. When swagger is down, don't start making massive decisions. Even though they might be the right or even necessary ones, you want to make absolute sure they're driven by truth, intention, and self-belief, not insecurity, fear, and pain. Until swagger returns, you won't be able to say that for sure. Step back, recover, and lick your soul wounds until you're feeling even just a little bit stronger again. When you feel the swagger start to creep back in, you'll be back on terra firma for life changes—but not before.

Love yourself through it. When my swagger took a nosedive, I felt incredibly sorry for myself, and I kept asking the universe, "Why, why, WHY?!" I noticed my language starting to include a lot of "shoulds." I should feel better. I should get over myself. I should know how to do this. I should be writing. I should be grateful. But I couldn't and I wasn't. Truth be told, I beat myself up a fair bit. Great strategy, huh—when life knocks you down, taking advantage and kicking the shit out of yourself?

Then I remembered the words of a smart therapist, who told me that when you're down for the count, vulnerable, and sad, try to treat yourself as you would your child—or, if you don't have kids, the way you would have wanted to be treated when you were one. Would you start ragging on them and giving them a lecture about pulling up their bootstraps and sucking it up? Hell to the no. (At least, I *hope* you wouldn't.) You would bend down and listen, cuddle, and reassure them. You'd give them ice cream for breakfast and let them stay home from school and watch cartoons all day. Maybe you'd put notes of encouragement in their lunch box and surprises under their pillow. And you'd tell them that you love them and that they're going to be OK. Well, I've got some news for ya. You can do all of that, and more, for yourself. Best of all, you don't need anyone's permission to do it.

Being in a place of true swagger is an ongoing journey. I remind myself every day that nobody is keeping score. "Oh, have you seen Leslie today? I'd give her a 3 on the swagger scale," said no one ever. By definition, having swagger means being vulnerable and honest about whatever your truth is.

Knowing how to bounce back or recover when life comes for your swagger is as important as knowing how to unleash it in the first place.

Knowing how to bounce back or recover when life comes for your swagger is as important as knowing how to unleash it in the first place. So, while you're standing in a shit storm, know that it won't melt you, and it definitely can't wash away your essence. Sure, you might get a little wet and stinky, but you'll dry off. And your tenacity, force of will, and truth will grow like hell as a result.

Today, my truth is that I'm more swagger-y than I was the day before. That's badass enough for me.

22

THE LAST WORD ON SWAGGER

SO THERE YOU HAVE IT. Everything I know on the subject of swagger.

For anyone reading this and still wondering whether they have the potential to live their best swagger life, I can tell you without a shadow of a doubt: you do.

People have often asked me, "How did you get so confident?" I tell them that confidence has nothing to do with it. Unlike Beyoncé, I didn't "wake up like this." Trust and believe that I spent many years living in the swaggerless darkness. It sucked big-time. So, I made the decision to climb out of that hole. The changes I went through were infinitesimal at times and epic at others. But over the years, they accumulated undeniably. Now, I just don't know any other way to *be* anymore. *That's* swagger.

No, it wasn't confidence that did it. It was courage. Just like everyone else on their swagger journey, I got sucked into persona, failed in my ambition, got knocked back by insecurity, was paralyzed by fear, and nearly drowned in pools of pain. But what I learned at every hurdle was that I alone had the power to pull up, achieve, push on, let go, and swim as if my life depended on it. Because it *did* depend on it if I wanted the *real* me to be free.

Today, what I get to experience, all the highs and lows of it, is fully mine. I am a product of my own authentic making, and no one can even begin to mess with that. True to the quote I have hanging in my guest bathroom, my attitude has become, "Fuck 'em if they can't take a joke." While I may take my contribution to the world very seriously, I try not to take *myself* quite as seriously. Now I laugh at my screwups and negative brain flares. "There I go," I say to myself. "Even after all these years, that shit's still in my head." I just forge on, with my truth, intention, and self-belief carving a path before me. Let me tell you, it makes life a helluva lot easier to navigate, especially the rocky parts.

Here's my wish for you, and the secret reason I wrote this book in the first place.

I know you have it in you. I know the real you is gorgeous, honest, powerful, and utterly amazing. Your swagger is just waiting and watching until you have the courage to free it. You are in *every* story that's been told here.

So do it. Be brave. Take your steps. Work through your blockers. Speak your fucking truth. Find the integrity in your intention and believe, believe, believe, even when others don't. Make swagger your reality. You deserve it.

I leave the final words to the inimitable Little Richard, who said, "I'm not conceited. I'm convinced."

So ends my work here. Yours is just beginning.

ACKNOWLEDGMENTS

WRITING A BOOK takes a freakin' village. You need people to listen, read, question, contribute, comment, and celebrate with you. I didn't know the half of it until I wrote this one. There are so many of you to thank and countless others whom I will no doubt forget to acknowledge, but I hope and trust that in true swagger style, you know who you are.

First and foremost, to all of the people who shared their stories for this book—it simply would not exist without your vulnerability, trust, and truth. You have given so much of yourselves in order to help the world find their swagger. I hope this makes you all very, very proud. I truly love and respect every single one of you!

To Andrea Positano: You and me, kid, from the start. You've seen it all and loved me unconditionally for it and through it. You are, quite simply, the best.

To Amanda Lewis, editor extraordinaire: Without your special sauce, this swagger would never have tasted so sweet. Thank you for letting *me* shine through the words.

To Jeffrey Shaw, my best Judy: Thank you for holding my hand and skipping through all of the hard parts with me—and then some.

To Sharon Hobson: Thank you for always bringing your A game to my voice and vision. Best wingwoman ever!

To Laura Gassner Otting, aka LGO: For paving the way, sharing your truth, intention, and self-belief, and for always reminding me that I, too, could be limitless—thank you.

To Ron Tite: My brother from another mother. You've inspired me through your fearless mastery of everything you've ever turned your hand to. You told me that if you could write a book, so could I. Then, I said, "Ha." Now, I say, "Thank you."

To Mike Alden: Thank you for being a relentless badass and helping to make my dreams come true. You promised, and you delivered.

To Robin Kershaw: My secret weapon. Your eyes, brain, and heart made this book so much better. Thank you for believing in me for so, so long.

To Melissa Agnes: My sister from another mister. Thank you for always being right there by my side when I needed you most, least, and every time in between.

To Virgil Barrow: Thank you for letting me "pray at the church of Virg" in my times of need. You are the living embodiment of swagger, my dear, dear friend.

To Lydia Saullo, Morgan Klein-MacNeil, and Eglys Vera: Thank you for being an unending source of support and believing without a doubt that the corporate world wanted and *needed* swagger. You all helped make it real.

To Liane Davey: For being my voice of reason, measure, and sanity while still reminding me in the end, "Do *you*, girl." You are a true supporter of all things swagger.

To Phil Jones: Thank you for listening, laughing, subtitling, and believing in and with me.

To Trena White: You are the "soulful co-author" of this book. Without your rock-solid belief and your swagger dance, this never would have happened. Thank you.

To my daddy, George Miechowsky: Thank you for having my back from day one. And I mean day one. Your unwavering love and support gave me the courage to take on the world. And I sure as hell did.

To my *real* sister, Erica Ehm: Thank you for seeing me, knowing me, and being utterly blasé about my writing this book because, "of *course* you're writing a book!" (Not to mention for sharing your cottage to write it in.) We've been through it all together and come out the other side better for it. Bubby and Min till the end!

To my mother, Evelyn Hannon, aka Journeywoman: You may not have lived to see it, but you are alive in every word. You were and will always be my mentor, my true north, and the original swagger queen. My self-belief is a by-product of your love.

To my crazy kids, Lotus and Bex: This mother could not be prouder of how 100% real you both are. Never lose your swagger, my beautiful girls.

Lastly, but mostly, to my husband, Russ: I've always said that nothing is real without you, and it's never been truer than right now. You are, quite simply, my everything. Thank you for loving and supporting me and never, ever doubting. I'm in love with you.

NOTES

1   See Daniel Campbell-Meiklejohn, Arndis Simonsen, Chris D. Frith, and
    Nathaniel D. Daw, "Independent Neural Computation of Value from
    Other People's Confidence," *Journal of Neuroscience* 37, no. 3 (2017): 673–
    84, doi.org/10.1523/JNEUROSCI.4490-15.2016.

2   Alex Lickerman, *The Undefeated Mind: On the Science of Constructing an
    Indestructible Self* (Deerfield Beach, FL: Health Communications, Inc., 2012).

3   Justin Kruger and David Dunning, "Unskilled and Unaware of It: How
    Difficulties in Recognizing One's Own Incompetence Lead to Inflated
    Self-Assessments," *Journal of Personality and Social Psychology* 77, no. 6
    (1999): 1121–34, doi.org/10.1037/0022-3514.77.6.1121.

4   Elliot Aronson, Ben Willerman, and Joanne Floyd, "The Effect of a
    Pratfall on Increasing Interpersonal Attractiveness," *Psychonomic
    Science* 4 (1966): 227–28, doi.org/10.3758/BF03342263.

5   Silvia Helena Cardoso, "Transcending the Tribal Mind," *Cérebro & Mente*
    [Brain & Mind], cerebromente.org.br/n09/tribal_i.htm.

6   Archy O. de Berker, Robb B. Rutledge, Christoph Mathys, Louise Marshall,
    Gemma F. Cross, Raymond J. Dolan, and Sven Bestmann, "Computations
    of Uncertainty Mediate Acute Stress Responses in Humans," *Nature
    Communications* 7, art. no. 10996 (2016), doi.org/10.1038/ncomms1099.

7   Wikipedia, s.v. "Parrhesia," en.wikipedia.org/w/index.php?title=
    Parrhesia&oldid=965948385.

8   Gilad Feldman, Huiwen Lian, Michal Kosinski, and David Stillwell, "Frankly, We Do Give a Damn: The Relationship between Profanity and Honesty," *Social Psychology and Personality Science* 8, no. 7 (2017): 816–26, doi.org/10.1177/1948550616681055.

9   Tommy Hawkins, "Bad Words: People Who Curse and Swear May Actually Have Higher Verbal Intelligence," Medical Daily, *The Grapevine* (blog), January 11, 2016, medicaldaily.com/bad-words-people-who-curse-and-swear-may-actually-have-higher-verbal-intelligence-368852; see also Kristin L. Jay and Timothy B. Jay, "Taboo Word Fluency and Knowledge of Slurs and General Pejoratives: Deconstructing the Poverty-of-Vocabulary Myth," *Language Sciences* 52 (2015): 251–59, doi.org/10.1016/j.langsci.2014.12.003.

10 "Swearing at Work: The Mixed Outcomes of Profanity," *Journal of Managerial Psychology* (April 2016): 1–26, openresearch.lsbu.ac.uk/download/324428ef48c9541e81d0ca6fef1373e8d3b83aea350c0a0399208cc0ce74118e/337628/Swearing%20at%20Work.pdf.

11 Fun fact: this quote is usually attributed to the late, great Maya Angelou, but it's really from Carl W. Buehner, who was a high-level official in The Church of Jesus Christ of Latter-day Saints. See Quote Investigator, quoteinvestigator.com/2014/04/06/they-feel/#return-note-8611-1.

12 "The Role of Emotion in Memory," About Memory (website), memory-key.com/memory/emotion; Johns Hopkins Medical Institutions, "Why Emotionally Charged Events Are So Memorable," *ScienceDaily*, October 7, 2007, sciencedaily.com/releases/2007/10/071004121045.htm.

13 Stephen G. Post, "Altruism, Happiness, and Health: It's Good to Be Good," *International Journal of Behavioral Medicine* 12 (2005): 66–77, doi.org/10.1207/s15327558ijbm1202_4.

ABOUT THE AUTHOR

Virgil Barrow

FORMER TV HOST and advertising creative director turned training guru, Leslie Ehm has spent decades traveling the globe with her award-winning company Combustion, working with executives and teams from top organizations like Google, Disney, PepsiCo, TD Bank, Uber, and more. She's turned technologists into creative forces, bankers into storytellers, and has brought a serious dose of badassery to boardrooms everywhere.

Fueled by her unrelenting passion to unleash human potential, Leslie is now a speaker, author, and swagger coach who's been called "better than therapy," "a rock star," "an ass-kicker," "a force of nature," and even "a witch."

SPREAD THE SWAGGER LOVE

Wouldn't the world be better if everyone had more swagger in their lives? You can help make that happen in a few easy ways.

1 **Write a five-star, kick-ass book review on your favorite bookseller site.** What you say matters and helps to spread the word!

2 **Join the Swagger Collective at LeslieEhm.com.** It's a direct way to get even more exclusive swagger love and learnings.

3 **Consider buying a copy of *Swagger* for everyone on your team or your organization.** Contact me about bulk discounts and special offers. I can make you a custom edition, even including a foreword from your Chief Swagger Officer or with your organization's branding. And depending on your buy, I'll provide you with other cool swagger perks like a custom keynote, virtual Swagger Q&A, complimentary swagger coaching, book signings, and more!

4 **Looking to infuse your next live or virtual event with some major swagger?** Invite me to speak and I promise to bring it big-time. My Swagger keynote will show your audience how to both unlock and unleash their personal brand of swagger as well as infuse it into their work culture, with an irresistible combination of unbridled energy, expertise, humor, and insight. Plus we can arrange for all of your participants to get a copy of my book!

5 **Swagger training or coaching?** Yes, that's a thing and I'm the woman to do it. My in-person or virtual swagger programs will unleash the best in your people—guaranteed.

6 **Gift this book to someone you love.** Friends don't let friends drive through life without swagger.

7 **Follow me on all the social platforms.** Get your regular dose of real talk, inspiration, laughs, insights, and general badassness.

8 **Share your #SwaggerMoment on social media.** Posting your progress with this hashtag is the perfect way to celebrate, reinforce, and share your own swagger journey. I'll be following along, commenting and celebrating with you.

With love and swagger,

Leslie E

Leslie Ehm

✉ Swagger@LeslieEhm.com   🌐 LeslieEhm.com
📷 @LeslieEhmSpeaks   🐦 @LeslieEhm
in @LeslieEhm   f @LeslieEhmSpeaks

Printed in Great Britain
by Amazon